As Always

Norma Fleming Murray

Good Food Means Bountiful Love

As Always

Recipes and Remembrances from Norma's

Norma Fleming Murray

As Always
Recipes and Remembrances from Norma's

Published by Norma's Potpourri Café, Inc.
Norma Fleming Murray, President
Betsy Kinney Daniels, Cookbook Project Manager

Copyright © 2002 by
Norma's Potpourri Café, Inc.

Norma's On the Run
28 North Palafox Street
Pensacola, Florida 32501
Telephone 1-850-434-8646
Fax 1-850-934-9586
E-mail normascookbook@earthlink.net

ISBN: 0-9722311-0-2

Edited, Designed, and Manufactured by

CommunityClassics™

An imprint of

FRP

P.O. Box 305142
Nashville, Tennessee 37230
(800) 358-0560

Manufactured in the United States of America
First Printing: 2002
10,000 copies

Contents

Did you enjoy your lunch today?

*As usual…Always do…As always…*What an affirmation of a job well done! I was flattered—and humbled—as I asked the post-lunch question and consistently received the same answer. Thus was born the title of my cookbook—

As Always

And since Norma's is so much more than just good food and great people, after fourteen years and so many customers, the stories I have to tell! Thank you, Pensacola, for welcoming me into your hearts and stomachs. Thank you ladies—Sharon, Joneida, Kathie, and Karen; Stacey, Stella, Pat, Priscilla, Norma Jean, Queenie, and Destiny—my everyday staff that is anything but ordinary! Thank you Betsy for keeping this project on track.

Most importantly, thank you to my family—Patrick, Meghan, and Caitlin—for the faith and patience you had in my dream. No one could love you more! How fortunate I have been to experience success doing what I enjoyed most. A childhood hobby transformed into a life's work. My recipes abound; my stories are plenty; my gratitude is unending. I hope you will enjoy *As Always* as much as I have.

As Always,
Norma

Introduction

The most important words in most relationships are "I love you" and "I need you." Although these were words I heard often during our fourteen years of marriage, the most important words I heard were spoken by my husband, Patrick, in February, 1986. Unknown to him or anyone else, I stood in line on Garden Street to apply for a job with D. H. Holmes Company of New Orleans, Louisiana. After two days in line, I sat across from a job counselor and was told that my background did not prepare me for the job I was interested in. After seven years of teaching and seven years of being a full-time, stay-at-home mom, I was bored! I wanted more. I intended to apply for a part-time sales job at the new store. But since my eyesight was keen and my spatial recognition high, I "upside-down" read the floor plan of the new D. H. Holmes store. A café—my cup of tea! Or so I thought.

When I told the interviewer that I wanted to apply for the job of cook in the kitchen, he chuckled and told me I was overqualified (M.S., Education) and underprepared (no culinary degree). I boldly informed him that I could do anything if someone was willing to teach me. Much to my surprise, I was hired.

When I rushed into my husband's office to tell him the news, he was shocked! But he spoke the most important words of our marriage—"If this is what you want to do, I'll help you. It's your turn now!" No finer words of love were ever spoken. Our family suddenly had to adjust to a Doctor-Daddy and Cooking-Mama. Our daughters, Meghan and Caitlin, learned early on about cooperation, juggling schedules, being flexible, and pursuing your dreams. Our daughters learned well.

About Norma's

Pleople are attracted to Norma's cafés for the delicious homemade-from-scratch gourmet food and unique ambience, but they keep coming back because they realize that Norma's is more than just a place to eat. The cozy cafés filled with easy laughter reflect Norma's gentle charm and make every meal a special occasion.

Café

Dillard's Cordova Mall
5100 North Ninth Avenue
Pensacola, Florida 32503

On the Run

Downtown Pensacola
28 North Palafox Street
Pensacola, Florida 32501

By the Bay

Gulf Power Corporate Headquarters
500 Bayfront Parkway
Pensacola, Florida 32501

Salads
As Usual

Norma's Chicken Salad

¹/₄ cup chicken base
¹/₄ cup lemon juice
¹/₂ gallon mayonnaise
8 cups chopped cooked chicken
2 cups diced celery
Field greens
Toasted almonds

For the salad dressing, combine the chicken base, lemon juice and mayonnaise in a large bowl and mix well. Chill until serving time.

For the salad, add the chicken and celery to the salad dressing and mix well. Serve over field greens. Sprinkle with toasted almonds.

Yield: 10 to 12 servings

For Norma's Baked Chicken Salad, follow the salad dressing recipe. Add the chicken, celery, ¹/₂ cup chopped onion and ¹/₂ cup toasted almonds. Spread the mixture in an 8×10-inch baking pan. Combine 2 cups crushed potato chips and 1 cup shredded Cheddar cheese in a bowl and mix well. Sprinkle on top of the chicken mixture. Bake at 350 degrees for 25 minutes or until the topping is browned.

The most popular chicken salad item on the menu at Norma's is the "Ben Salad." "Ben" is my friend, my first accountant, my mentor. One negative word from Ben in 1988 and there would have been no Norma's. Thank you, Ben!

Champagne Chicken Salad

4 cups mayonnaise
3/4 cup sugar
1/2 cup Champagne
1/2 cup white vinegar
4 cups chopped cooked chicken
2 cups chopped red apples
2 cups chopped pears
Field greens
Toasted walnuts
Crumbled bleu cheese

For the salad dressing, combine the mayonnaise, sugar, Champagne and vinegar in a blender. Process until blended.

For the salad, combine the salad dressing, chicken, apples and pears in a bowl and mix well. Serve over field greens. Sprinkle with walnuts and cheese.

Yield: 8 to 10 servings

 "I don't think so," was my daughter's reply to her middle school teacher's request for a favorite recipe from Norma's. When the teacher realized Caitlin's mom was "Norma," she assumed she could finally get a coveted recipe for chicken salad. Caitlin very politely informed the teacher that Mama's recipes were going to help put her through college and possibly provide an inheritance one day. Quickly translated, this young lady was not giving away Mom's secrets. You go girl!

Marinated Chicken Salad

2 cups red wine vinegar
2 cups olive oil
2 cups vegetable oil
1 teaspoon garlic powder
1 teaspoon seasoned salt
8 cups chopped cooked chicken
1 large red onion, sliced
1 cup green olives
1 cup black olives
Red and green bell pepper strips
12 mushrooms, thickly sliced
3 cans artichoke hearts, drained, quartered

For the salad dressing, combine the vinegar, olive oil, vegetable oil, garlic powder and seasoned salt in a food processor. Process until blended.

For the salad, combine the salad dressing and chicken in a bowl. Chill, covered, until serving time to marinate the chicken. Add the onion, green olives, black olives, bell peppers, mushrooms and artichoke hearts to the chicken mixture and mix well.

Yield: 12 servings

Chicken and Artichoke Salad

1½ cups olive oil
½ cup white vinegar
½ teaspoon garlic powder
½ teaspoon dry mustard
1 teaspoon seasoned salt
1 teaspoon black pepper
⅓ cup lime juice
4 cups chopped cooked chicken
½ cup chopped celery
½ cup torn fresh spinach
2 cups chopped drained canned artichoke hearts
2 cups cooked penne pasta
Field greens
Freshly grated Parmesan cheese

For the salad dressing, combine the olive oil, vinegar, garlic powder, dry mustard, seasoned salt, black pepper and lime juice in a food processor. Process until well blended.

For the salad, combine the salad dressing, chicken, celery, spinach, artichoke hearts and pasta in a bowl and mix well. Serve over field greens. Sprinkle with cheese.

Yield: 8 to 10 servings

Chicken Pasta Salad

2 cups vegetable oil
2¹/₂ cups red wine vinegar
1 cup honey
1 teaspoon garlic powder
1 tablespoon ginger
¹/₂ teaspoon seasoned salt
3 cups cooked rotini pasta
2 cups chopped cooked chicken
¹/₂ cup sliced zucchini
¹/₂ cup sliced yellow squash
¹/₂ cup chopped carrots
¹/₂ cup cauliflower flowerettes
¹/₂ cup broccoli flowerettes
Field greens
Sunflower seeds

For the salad dressing, combine the oil, vinegar, honey, garlic powder, ginger and seasoned salt in a food processor. Process until well blended.

For the salad, combine the salad dressing, pasta, chicken, zucchini, yellow squash, carrots, cauliflower and broccoli in a bowl and mix well. Serve over field greens. Sprinkle with sunflower seeds.

Yield: 8 to 10 servings

Curried Chicken Salad

1/2 cup mayonnaise
1 cup sour cream
2 tablespoons lemon juice
1 1/2 teaspoons curry powder
1 tablespoon chopped fresh parsley
1 teaspoon tarragon
1 tablespoon Grey Poupon mustard
4 cups chopped cooked chicken
1 cup diced celery
1 cup golden raisins
1/2 cup toasted almonds

For the salad dressing, combine the mayonnaise, sour cream, lemon juice, curry powder, parsley, tarragon and Grey Poupon mustard in a food processor. Process until well blended.

For the salad, combine the salad dressing, chicken, celery and raisins in a bowl and mix well. Chill, covered, for 2 hours. Sprinkle with the almonds just before serving.

Yield: 8 to 10 servings

Mandarin Chicken and Rice Salad

1¹/₂ cups olive oil
¹/₂ cup white vinegar
¹/₂ teaspoon garlic powder
¹/₂ teaspoon dry mustard
1 teaspoon seasoned salt
1 teaspoon white pepper
¹/₂ cup orange juice concentrate
4 cups chopped cooked chicken
1 cup chopped celery
1 box garden-blend rice, cooked
¹/₂ cup shredded carrots
¹/₂ cup drained canned mandarin oranges
Field greens
Mixed nuts

For the salad dressing, combine the olive oil, vinegar, garlic powder, dry mustard, seasoned salt, white pepper and orange juice concentrate in a food processor. Process until well blended.

For the salad, combine the salad dressing, chicken, celery, rice, carrots and mandarin oranges in a bowl and mix well. Serve over field greens. Sprinkle with mixed nuts.

Yield: 8 to 10 servings

Oriental Chicken Salad

1¹/₂ cups vegetable oil
²/₃ cup honey
²/₃ cup white vinegar
1 cup soy sauce
2 teaspoons dry mustard
8 cups chopped cooked chicken
2 cups drained sliced water chestnuts
2 cups drained chopped pineapple

For the salad dressing, combine the oil, honey, vinegar, soy sauce and dry mustard in a food processor. Process until well blended.

For the salad, combine the salad dressing and chicken in a large bowl. Chill, covered, until serving time to marinate the chicken. Add the water chestnuts and pineapple and toss to mix well.

Yield: 10 to 12 servings

Jambalaya Salad

2 cups chopped onions
1 cup chopped green bell
   pepper
1 cup chopped red bell
   pepper
1 cup chopped green onions
$1/3$ cup olive oil
2 teaspoons crushed red
   pepper
$1^1/2$ tablespoons thyme
6 bay leaves
$1/2$ gallon water

$1/3$ cup chicken base
6 cups rice
2 cups chopped celery
4 cups chopped cooked
   chicken
3 cups diced ham
3 cups cooked peeled
   shrimp
Lettuce leaves
Tomato wedges
Fresh fruit
Mustard Vinaigrette (page 29)

Sauté the onions, bell peppers and green onions in the olive oil in a skillet over medium-high heat until tender but not browned. Add the crushed red pepper, thyme and bay leaves.

Cook until fragrant, stirring constantly. Add the water, chicken base and rice. Bring to a boil. Reduce the heat to low. Cook until the water is absorbed, stirring occasionally. Remove the bay leaves. Remove to a bowl. Chill, covered, until serving time.

Add the celery, chicken, ham and shrimp to the rice mixture and mix well. Serve on beds of lettuce with tomato wedges, fresh fruit and Mustard Vinaigrette.

Yield: 12 servings

Burgundy Beef Salad

3 cups zesty Italian salad dressing
1¹/₂ cups burgundy wine
¹/₄ cup beef base
2 cups cooked lean beef strips
1 cup sliced zucchini
1 cup sliced yellow squash
¹/₂ cup sliced red onion
¹/₂ cup sliced black olives
¹/₂ cup sliced green olives
Field greens
Red or green bell pepper strips

For the salad dressing, combine the Italian salad dressing, burgundy wine and beef base in a food processor. Process until well blended.

For the salad, combine the salad dressing, beef, zucchini, yellow squash, red onion, black olives and green olives in a bowl and mix well. Serve over field greens. Top with bell pepper strips.

Yield: 8 to 10 servings

Marinated Beef and Mushroom Salad

1¹/₂ cups vegetable oil
1¹/₂ cups red wine vinegar
2 cups Grey Poupon mustard
¹/₂ teaspoon garlic powder
3 cups cooked lean beef strips
3 cups fresh mushrooms, thickly sliced
Spinach
Sun sprouts

For the salad dressing, combine the oil, vinegar, Grey Poupon mustard and garlic powder in a food processor. Process until well blended.

For the salad, combine the salad dressing, beef strips and mushrooms in a bowl and mix well. Serve over spinach. Top with sun sprouts.

Yield: 8 to 10 servings

Broccoli, Ham and Berry Salad

4 cups mayonnaise
$3/4$ cup sugar
$3/4$ cup white vinegar
3 cups diced ham
3 cups broccoli flowerettes
$1/2$ cup diced red onion
$1/2$ cup shredded carrots
1 cup dried cranberries
Field greens
Sunflower seeds

For the salad dressing, combine the mayonnaise, sugar and vinegar in a large bowl and mix well.

For the salad, combine the salad dressing, ham, broccoli, onion, carrots and dried cranberries in a bowl and mix well. Serve over field greens. Sprinkle with sunflower seeds.

Yield: 8 to 10 servings

Turkey and Wild Rice Salad

1¹/₂ cups olive oil
¹/₂ cup white vinegar
¹/₂ teaspoon garlic powder
¹/₂ teaspoon dry mustard
1 teaspoon seasoned salt
1 teaspoon black pepper
¹/₄ cup lemon juice
4 cups chopped cooked turkey breast
1 cup chopped celery
1 cup shredded carrots
1 box wild rice, cooked
Field greens
Mixed nuts

For the salad dressing, combine the olive oil, vinegar, garlic powder, dry mustard, seasoned salt, black pepper and lemon juice in a food processor. Process until well blended.

For the salad, combine the salad dressing, turkey, celery, carrots and wild rice in a bowl and mix well. Serve over field greens. Sprinkle with mixed nuts.

Yield: 8 to 10 servings

Dill Shrimp and Rice Salad

1¹/₂ cups mayonnaise
2 cups sour cream
1 tablespoon chopped fresh parsley
2 tablespoons dill weed
¹/₂ tablespoon lemon juice
¹/₂ tablespoon seasoned salt
3 cups boiled shrimp, cooled, peeled
1 cup chopped celery
1 cup cooked wild rice
Field greens
Tomato slices
Cucumber slices

For the salad dressing, combine the mayonnaise, sour cream, parsley, dill weed, lemon juice and seasoned salt in a large bowl and mix well.

For the salad, add the shrimp, celery and wild rice to the dressing and mix well. Chill, covered, for 2 hours. Serve over field greens. Garnish with tomato slices and cucumber slices.

Yield: 8 to 10 servings

Shrimp and Artichoke Salad

4 cups cooked peeled shrimp
3 cans artichoke hearts, drained, chopped
1 cup sliced green olives
3 cups Parmesan-pepper salad dressing
Lettuce leaves
Tomato wedges
Lemon wedges
Paprika

Combine the shrimp, artichoke hearts, green olives and salad dressing in a bowl and toss lightly to mix.

Serve on lettuce leaves on salad plates with tomato wedges and lemon wedges. Sprinkle with paprika.

Yield: 12 servings

For Crab and Artichoke Salad, substitute 1 pound lump crab meat for the shrimp and 1 cup sliced black olives for the green olives.

Shrimp and Shells Salad

3 cups mayonnaise
$1^1/_2$ cups sour cream
$^1/_2$ teaspoon seasoned salt
1 teaspoon white pepper
1 tablespoon Tabasco sauce
1 tablespoon lemon juice
2 tablespoons seafood base
2 cups peeled cooked shrimp
2 cups cooked pasta shells
$^1/_2$ cup chopped celery
$^1/_2$ cup diced tomatoes
Field greens
Paprika

For the salad dressing, combine the mayonnaise, sour cream, seasoned salt, white pepper, Tabasco sauce, lemon juice and seafood base in a food processor. Process until well blended.

For the salad, combine the salad dressing, shrimp, pasta, celery and tomatoes in a bowl and mix well. Serve over field greens. Sprinkle with paprika.

Yield: 8 to 10 servings

Mexican Fiesta Salad

2 cups zesty Italian salad dressing
$1/2$ cup lime juice
$1^{1}/_{2}$ cups garden salsa
1 tablespoon beef base
2 cans black beans, drained
1 can corn, drained
1 medium red bell pepper, diced
2 green onions, chopped
2 cups drained cooked ground beef
8 to 10 tortilla salad shells
Mixed greens
Diced tomatoes
Sour cream
Shredded Monterey Jack cheese
Shredded Cheddar cheese

For the salad dressing, combine the Italian salad dressing, lime juice, salsa and beef base in a large bowl and mix well.

For the salad, add the black beans, corn, bell pepper, green onions and ground beef to the dressing and mix well. Serve in the tortilla salad shells with mixed greens and diced tomatoes. Top with dollops of sour cream. Sprinkle with Monterey Jack and Cheddar cheeses.

Yield: 8 to 10 servings

Tortellini Salad

2 cups vegetable oil
2 cups red wine vinegar
$1/2$ teaspoon garlic powder
$1/2$ teaspoon dry mustard
1 teaspoon salt
1 tablespoon basil
$1/4$ cup sugar
$1/2$ cup tomato paste
1 package frozen tricolor
   tortellini, thawed
1 can chopped artichoke
   hearts, drained

2 cups sliced mushrooms
1 cup diced celery
$1/2$ cup sliced black olives
1 cup sliced zucchini
1 cup sliced yellow squash
Lettuce leaves
Freshly grated Parmesan
   cheese
Tomato wedges
Grapes
Croutons

For the salad dressing, combine the oil, vinegar, garlic powder, dry mustard, salt, basil, sugar and tomato paste in a food processor. Process until well blended.

For the salad, combine the salad dressing, pasta, artichoke hearts, mushrooms, celery, black olives, zucchini and yellow squash in a bowl and mix well. Serve on beds of lettuce. Sprinkle with cheese. Serve with tomato wedges, grapes and croutons.

Yield: 10 to 12 servings

Norma's Poppy Seed Salad Dressing

3 cups sugar
1$\frac{1}{2}$ tablespoons dry mustard
1 tablespoon salt
2 cups white vinegar
$\frac{1}{2}$ cup finely chopped onion
4 cups vegetable oil
1 cup poppy seeds

Combine the sugar, dry mustard, salt, vinegar, onion, oil and poppy seeds in a bowl and mix until smooth and thickened.

Yield: 8 cups

For Burgundy Poppy Seed Salad Dressing, decrease the amount of vinegar to 1$\frac{1}{2}$ cups and add $\frac{1}{2}$ cup burgundy wine.

Mustard Vinaigrette

2 whole eggs
4 egg yolks, or $2/3$ cup egg substitute
2 tablespoons dry mustard
1 teaspoon salt
1 tablespoon black pepper
1 cup red wine vinegar
4 cups olive oil

Combine the eggs, egg yolks, dry mustard, salt and black pepper in a food processor. Add the vinegar and olive oil gradually, processing constantly. Process until well blended.

Yield: 6 cups

Muffaletta Salad Dressing

1/2 cup green onions
1 cup coarsely chopped celery
2 cups black olives
2 cups green olives
1/2 cup olive oil
2 teaspoons oregano
2 teaspoons basil
2 teaspoons thyme
1 tablespoon black pepper
1 teaspoon garlic powder
1 tablespoon lemon juice
1/4 teaspoon cayenne pepper
2 cups mayonnaise
1/4 cup wine vinegar

Combine the green onions, celery, black olives and green olives in a food processor. Process until finely chopped. Add the olive oil, oregano, basil, thyme, black pepper, garlic powder, lemon juice, cayenne pepper, mayonnaise and vinegar and process until smooth.

May be used for sandwiches, heated and served over baked ham or chicken or served cold over chilled pasta.

Yield: 4 cups

"That's My Norma"

"Hurry up, Dr. Murray. I'm supposed to go to Norma's for lunch today. You know, if I'm not there by 11:15, I'll have to wait." The new mom was trying to complete her first outing at the pediatrician's office with lunch at Norma's. Little did she know that the two were related. Dr. Murray looked at the new mom and simply said, "That's my Norma."

Of all the titles I may ever have, I'm most proud of being "his Norma."

Roses are red,

Violets are blue,

You finished the first day,

We're so very, very proud of you!

Love,
–Meghan and Caitlin
August 1, 1988

MAMA

Soups
Always Do

Norma's Chicken Soup

2 cups chopped onions
4 cups chopped celery
1/4 cup (1/2 stick) butter
1/2 cup flour
1 cup chicken base
1 teaspoon white pepper
1 1/2 gallons water
4 cups finely chopped cooked chicken

Sauté the onions and celery in the butter in a stockpot over medium-high heat until light brown. Add the flour and blend well. Cook over medium heat for 10 minutes, stirring constantly. Stir in the chicken base, white pepper and water. Bring to a boil. Boil for 30 minutes. Reduce the heat to low. Add the chicken and mix well.

Yield: 2 1/2 gallons

For Chicken Noodle Soup, add 2 beaten eggs to the hot chicken stock and mix well. Add 2 cups broken fettuccini and mix well. Cook for 45 minutes or until pasta is tender. Stir in desired amount of chopped fresh parsley.

For Chicken and Rice Soup, add some hot chicken stock to 2 beaten eggs in a bowl. Stir egg mixture into stock. Add 3 cups rice. Cook for 30 minutes or until rice is tender. Stir in desired amount of chopped fresh parsley.

For Chicken and Wild Rice Soup, add 1 box wild rice with seasonings to the hot chicken stock and mix well. Cook for 30 minutes or until rice is tender.

For Chicken Pasta Soup, add 1/2 cup tomato paste to the hot chicken stock and mix well. Stir in 4 cups rotini pasta. Cook for 45 minutes or until pasta is tender.

For Chicken Vegetable Soup, add 1 large bag frozen vegetables to the hot chicken stock and mix well. Cook for 30 minutes.

Norma's Chicken Soup (continued)

For Chicken and Bows Soup, add 2 cups heavy cream to the hot chicken stock and mix well. Stir in 4 cups bow tie pasta. Cook for 40 minutes or until pasta is tender.

For Chicken Chowder, decrease the amount of water in the chicken stock to 1 gallon and add 1 gallon milk. Add 5 pounds diced potatoes to the hot chicken stock and mix well. Cook for 45 minutes or until potatoes are tender. Stir in desired amount of chopped fresh parsley.

For Cream of Chicken Soup, decrease the amount of water in the chicken stock to 1 gallon. Add 4 cups heavy cream to the hot chicken stock and mix well. Stir in 1 teaspoon white pepper. Cook for 30 minutes.

For Chicken Florentine Soup, add 2 cups heavy cream to the hot chicken stock and mix well. Stir in 1 package frozen spinach soufflé, thawed, 2 bay leaves and $1/2$ teaspoon white pepper. Cook for 30 minutes. Remove and discard bay leaves before serving.

For Chicken Italiano Soup, decrease the amount of water in the chicken stock to 1 gallon. Add 1 large can chopped tomatoes, $1/4$ cup zesty Italian dressing, 3 cups broken fettuccini, $1/2$ teaspoon basil, $1/2$ teaspoon thyme, $1/2$ teaspoon garlic powder and $1/2$ teaspoon oregano to the hot chicken stock and mix well. Cook for 45 minutes or until pasta is tender.

 Name that soup! The hardest part of creative cooking is naming the end result. Often it takes longer to "name the soup" than to make it! If you don't find a favorite soup listed in As Always, it may be because it's impossible to duplicate. Many, many soups are made of leftover specials or "a little of this, a little of that."

Norma's Seafood Gumbo

1 cup (2 sticks) margarine
1 cup bacon drippings
2 cups flour
3 cups chopped onions
3 cups chopped celery
2 cups chopped green bell
   peppers
1/2 cup (1 stick) margarine
3 gallons water
1 tablespoon garlic powder
4 bay leaves
1 tablespoon thyme

1/2 tablespoon black pepper
3/4 cup seafood base
2 large cans crushed
   tomatoes
1/2 cup filé powder
1 large bag frozen chopped
   okra
3 to 5 pounds uncooked
   shrimp, peeled
2 pounds claw crab meat
1/2 teaspoon cayenne pepper
Rice

For the roux, combine 1 cup margarine and the bacon drippings in a deep ovenproof pan. Cook at 400 degrees for 20 minutes or until dark brown. Remove from the oven. Whisk in the flour until the mixture is smooth. Cook in the oven until dark brown.

For the gumbo, sauté the onions, celery and bell peppers in 1/2 cup margarine in a large stockpot over medium-high heat until tender. Stir in the water, garlic powder, bay leaves, thyme, black pepper and seafood base. Cook over low heat for 40 minutes. Add the crushed tomatoes and mix well. Cook for 40 minutes. Add the roux and mix well. Whisk in the filé powder. Add the okra and mix well. Cook for 40 minutes. Stir in the shrimp, crab meat and cayenne pepper. Cook until thickened. Remove the bay leaves. Serve over rice.

Yield: 3 1/2 gallons

"What do you do with that huge pot?" a new employee asked. She was referring to the Groen 40-gallon steam pot bolted to the floor. In most cases we make gallons and gallons and gallons of Seafood Gumbo or soups. But on the occasion of our grand opening black-tie party in 1988, we filled that pot with ice and chilled our Champagne bottles in it. A tuxedoed waiter served glasses of Champagne as guests toured the kitchen. Champagne or Gumbo—Gumbo or Champagne—hard decision!

Cream of Artichoke Soup

4 cups chopped celery
4 cups chopped onions
6 cans chopped artichoke hearts, drained
$1/2$ cup (1 stick) butter
$1/2$ cup flour
1 cup chicken base
$1^1/2$ gallons water
$1/2$ gallon milk
2 quarts heavy cream
1 tablespoon thyme
1 tablespoon basil
1 teaspoon garlic powder
$1/2$ teaspoon white pepper
$1/2$ cup lemon juice
$1/2$ cup chopped fresh parsley

Sauté the celery, onions and artichoke hearts in the butter in a stockpot over medium-high heat until tender. Add the flour. Cook for 10 minutes, stirring constantly.

Add the chicken base and water and mix well. Bring to a boil. Stir in the milk and heavy cream. Add the thyme, basil, garlic powder and white pepper and mix well. Cook over low heat for 1 hour. Stir in the lemon juice and parsley.

Yield: 3 gallons

Cream of Celery Soup

2¹/₂ cups chopped onions
6 cups chopped celery
¹/₂ cup (1 stick) butter
¹/₂ cup flour
1 cup chicken base
1 gallon water
1 quart heavy cream
1¹/₂ tablespoons basil
¹/₂ tablespoon thyme
¹/₂ teaspoon garlic powder
1 teaspoon white pepper

Sauté the onions and celery in the butter in a stockpot over medium-high heat until tender. Add the flour. Cook for 10 minutes, stirring constantly.

Add the chicken base, water and heavy cream and mix well. Stir in the basil, thyme, garlic powder and white pepper. Cook over low heat for 1 hour.

Yield: 2 gallons

Potato Chowder

4 cups chopped celery
4 cups chopped onions
1/2 cup (1 stick) butter
1/2 cup flour
1 cup chicken base
1 gallon water
1/2 gallon milk

5 pounds frozen diced
   potatoes
1 quart heavy cream
1 teaspoon white pepper
1/2 teaspoon garlic powder
1/4 cup chopped fresh
   parsley

Sauté the celery and onions in the butter in a stockpot over medium-high heat until tender. Add the flour. Cook for 10 minutes, stirring constantly.

Add the chicken base, water, milk and potatoes and mix well. Cook until the potatoes are tender, stirring frequently. Stir in the heavy cream, white pepper, garlic powder and parsley. Cook for 20 minutes.

Yield: 2 gallons

For Sour Cream Potato Soup, omit the cream. Add 2 cups sour cream and blend well. Sprinkle with bacon bits.

For Ham and Potato Chowder, decrease the amount of chicken base to 1/3 cup. Add 1/3 cup ham base and 6 cups chopped ham.

For Cheesy Ham and Potato Chowder, add 2 large jars Cheez Whiz to Ham and Potato Chowder and blend well.

Cream of Tomato Soup

2 1/2 cups chopped onions
4 cups chopped celery
1/4 cup (1/2 stick) butter
1/2 cup flour
1 cup chicken base
1 gallon water
1 quart heavy cream
1/4 cup tomato paste

2 large cans crushed
  tomatoes
1 tablespoon basil
1 tablespoon thyme
1/2 tablespoon oregano
1/2 teaspoon garlic powder
1 teaspoon white pepper
3 bay leaves

Sauté the onions and celery in the butter in a stockpot over medium-high heat until tender. Add the flour. Cook for 10 minutes, stirring constantly. Add the chicken base, water, heavy cream, tomato paste and crushed tomatoes and mix well. Stir in the basil, thyme, oregano, garlic powder, white pepper and bay leaves. Cook over low heat for 1 hour.

Yield: 2 gallons

For Tomato Florentine Soup, add 1 large bag frozen chopped spinach. Cook until heated through.

For Tomato Vegetable Soup, omit the heavy cream and add 2 large bags frozen chopped vegetables. Cook until heated through.

For Italian Tomato Soup, add 1/2 cup zesty Italian salad dressing and 3 cups cooked penne pasta. Cook until heated through.

For Tomato Tortellini Soup, add 1 bag frozen cheese tortellini. Cook until tortellini is done.

Vegetable Soup

4 cups chopped celery
4 cups chopped onions
$1/4$ cup ($1/2$ stick) butter
$1/2$ cup flour
$1 1/2$ gallons water
$1/2$ cup ham base
$1/2$ cup chicken base
2 large cans crushed tomatoes
2 cups chopped ham
4 cups assorted vegetables
$1/2$ teaspoon white pepper
$1/2$ teaspoon garlic powder
2 bay leaves

Sauté the celery and onions in the butter in a stockpot over medium-high heat until tender. Add the flour. Cook for 10 minutes, stirring constantly.

Add the water, ham base, chicken base, crushed tomatoes, ham and vegetables and mix well. Stir in the white pepper, garlic powder and bay leaves. Cook over low heat for 1 hour or longer, stirring occasionally. Remove the bay leaves before serving.

Yield: 2 gallons

Creamy Corn Soup

2 cups chopped onions	3 packages frozen corn
4 cups chopped celery	soufflé, thawed
1/2 cup (1 stick) butter	1 teaspoon white pepper
1/2 cup flour	1/2 teaspoon garlic powder
1 gallon water	2 cups heavy cream
1 cup chicken base	(optional)
1/2 gallon milk	

Sauté the onions and celery in the butter in a stockpot over medium-high heat until tender. Add the flour. Cook for 10 minutes, stirring constantly.

Add the water, chicken base, milk and corn soufflé and mix well. Cook over low heat for 1 1/2 hours. Stir in the white pepper and garlic powder. Whisk in the heavy cream if soup separates or curdles. Cook for 20 minutes.

Yield: 2 gallons

For Pepper Corn Soup, sauté 1 cup chopped green bell pepper and 1 cup chopped red bell pepper with the onions and celery. Add 1 teaspoon crushed red pepper with the seasonings.

For Ham and Corn Soup, decrease the amount of chicken base to 1/3 cup. Add 1/3 cup ham base and 6 cups diced ham.

For Shrimp and Corn Soup, decrease the amount of chicken base to 1/2 cup. Add 1/2 cup seafood base and 6 cups peeled cooked shrimp.

Zucchini Carrot Soup

1 cup chopped onion
1 cup chopped celery
6 cups chopped zucchini
2 cups chopped carrots
$1/2$ cup (1 stick) butter
1 cup flour
1 gallon water
$1/3$ cup chicken base
2 quarts heavy cream
1 gallon milk
2 teaspoons tarragon
1 teaspoon marjoram
1 teaspoon white pepper
1 teaspoon dill weed

Sauté the onion, celery, zucchini and carrots in the butter in a stockpot over medium-high heat until tender. Add the flour. Cook for 10 minutes, stirring constantly.

Add the water, chicken base, heavy cream and milk. Stir in the tarragon, marjoram, white pepper and dill weed. Cook for 1 hour or longer.

Yield: $2^1/2$ gallons

Cream of Cauliflower Soup

2 cups chopped onions
2 cups chopped celery
8 cups chopped cauliflower
$1/2$ cup (1 stick) butter
1 cup flour
$1^1/2$ gallons water
$2/3$ cup chicken base
1 gallon milk
1 quart heavy cream
1 teaspoon garlic powder
1 teaspoon white pepper
1 teaspoon thyme

Sauté the onions, celery and cauliflower in the butter in a stockpot over medium-high heat until tender. Add the flour. Cook for 10 minutes, stirring constantly.

Add the water, chicken base, milk, heavy cream, garlic powder, white pepper and thyme and mix well. Cook for 1 hour or longer.

Yield: $2^1/2$ gallons

Cream of Spinach Soup

2 cups chopped celery
2 cups chopped onions
$1/4$ cup ($1/2$ stick) butter
$1/2$ cup flour
1 gallon water
$1/2$ cup chicken base
$1/2$ gallon milk
$1/2$ quart heavy cream
2 packages frozen spinach soufflé, thawed
2 bay leaves
$1/2$ teaspoon white pepper
$1/2$ teaspoon nutmeg
1 cup warm heavy cream (optional)

Sauté the celery and onions in the butter in a stockpot over medium-high heat until tender. Add the flour. Cook for 10 minutes, stirring constantly.

Add the water and chicken base and mix well. Bring to a boil over medium heat. Add the milk, heavy cream and spinach soufflé and mix well. Cook over low heat for 30 minutes; do not boil.

Stir in the bay leaves, white pepper and nutmeg. Cook for 35 to 40 minutes. Whisk in the warm heavy cream if soup separates or curdles. Cook for 20 minutes. Remove the bay leaves before serving.

Yield: 2 gallons

Cheesy Cauliflower Soup

2 cups chopped onions
1 tablespoon garlic powder
8 cups chopped cauliflower
1/2 cup (1 stick) butter
1 cup flour
2 packages cheese sauce mix
1 gallon water
1/2 cup chicken base

Sauté the onions, garlic powder and cauliflower in the butter in a stockpot over medium-high heat until tender. Add the flour. Cook for 10 minutes, stirring constantly.

Prepare the cheese sauce mix using the package directions. Add the water, chicken base and cheese sauce to the onion mixture and mix well. Cook until smooth and creamy, stirring frequently.

Yield: 3 gallons

Cream of Broccoli Soup

$^1/_2$ **cup chopped green onions**
8 cups chopped broccoli
$^1/_2$ **cup (1 stick) butter**
$^1/_2$ **cup flour**
1 gallon water
1 cup chicken base
$^1/_2$ **gallon milk**
1$^1/_2$ quarts heavy cream
$^1/_3$ **cup Grey Poupon mustard**

Sauté the green onions and broccoli in the butter in a stockpot over medium-high heat until tender. Add the flour. Cook for 10 minutes, stirring constantly.

Add the water and chicken base and mix well. Cook for 1 hour or longer. Add milk and heavy cream. Bring to a boil over medium heat. Stir in the Grey Poupon mustard.

Yield: 2 gallons

For Cheesy Broccoli Soup, omit the milk, cream and Grey Poupon mustard. Prepare 2 packages cheese sauce mix using the package directions. Add to the soup and mix well.

Mushroom Soup

1/2 cup chopped green onions
2 pounds mushrooms, sliced
1/4 cup (1/2 stick) butter
1/2 cup flour
1/2 cup chicken base
1 gallon water
1/2 gallon milk
1 quart heavy cream
2 bay leaves
1/2 tablespoon thyme
1 teaspoon white pepper
2 tablespoons lemon juice
1 teaspoon salt

Sauté the green onions and mushrooms in the butter in a stockpot over medium-high heat until tender. Stir in the flour. Cook for 10 minutes, stirring constantly.

Add the chicken base and water and mix well. Bring to a boil. Reduce the heat to low. Add the milk and heavy cream and mix well. Cook for 30 minutes. Stir in the bay leaves, thyme, white pepper, lemon juice and salt. Remove the bay leaves before serving.

Yield: 2 gallons

Onion Soup

5 pounds onions, chopped
1 tablespoon sugar
1 cup (2 sticks) butter
1 cup flour
2$1/2$ gallons water
1 cup beef base
$1/2$ cup chicken base
6 bay leaves
1 teaspoon white pepper
1 cup white wine
White cheeses

Sauté the onions and sugar in the butter in a stockpot over medium-high heat until the onions are tender. Add the flour. Cook for 10 minutes, stirring constantly.

Add the water, beef base and chicken base and mix well. Bring to a boil over medium heat. Cook for 1 hour. Stir in the bay leaves, white pepper and white wine. Cook for 20 minutes. Remove the bay leaves before serving. Serve with white cheeses.

Yield: 3 gallons

For Cream of Onion Soup, decrease the amount of water to 1$1/2$ gallons. Add $1/2$ gallon milk and 2 quarts heavy cream. Omit the white cheeses.

Beer Cheese Soup

1 cup (2 sticks) butter
1 cup flour
$1/2$ gallon water
$1/3$ cup chicken base
1 package cheese sauce mix
2 cans beer
2 tablespoons Worcestershire sauce

Melt the butter in a stockpot over medium heat. Stir in the flour. Cook until bubbly, stirring constantly. Add the water and chicken base and mix well. Cook for 10 minutes.

Prepare the cheese sauce mix using the package directions. Add the cheese sauce to the pot and whisk to mix well. Cook for 30 minutes. Add the beer and Worcestershire sauce and mix well. Cook over low heat for 10 to 15 minutes.

Yield: 1$1/2$ gallons

Seafood Bisque

1/2 cup chopped green bell pepper
1/2 cup chopped onion
1/2 cup chopped green onions
1/4 cup chopped fresh parsley
4 cups sliced fresh mushrooms
1/2 cup (1 stick) butter
1/4 cup flour

2 cups half-and-half
2 cups milk
1 gallon water
2 cups heavy cream
1/4 cup seafood base
1 teaspoon salt
1/4 teaspoon white pepper
2 1/2 pounds peeled shrimp
1 pound crab meat
1/2 cup dry sherry

Sauté the bell pepper, onion, green onions, parsley and mushrooms in the butter in a stockpot over medium-high heat until tender. Add the flour. Cook for 10 minutes, stirring constantly.

Add the half-and-half, milk, water, heavy cream and seafood base and mix well. Stir in the salt, white pepper, shrimp and crab meat. Cook for 35 to 40 minutes. Remove from the heat. Stir in the sherry.

Yield: 1 1/2 gallons

Crab Chowder

3 cups chopped celery
2 cups chopped green onions
$1/2$ cup chopped fresh parsley
$1/2$ cup (1 stick) butter
1 cup flour
$1^1/_2$ gallons water
$1/2$ cup seafood base
$1/2$ gallon milk
1 quart heavy cream
2 pounds claw crab meat
1 teaspoon white pepper

Sauté the celery, green onions and parsley in the butter in a stockpot over medium-high heat until tender. Add the flour. Cook for 10 minutes, stirring constantly.

Add the water, seafood base, milk and heavy cream and mix well. Cook over low heat for 45 minutes. Stir in the crab meat and white pepper. Cook for 20 minutes.

Yield: $2^1/_2$ gallons

Split Pea Soup

    2 cups chopped celery
    2 cups chopped onions
    $1/4$ cup ($1/2$ stick) butter
    2 pounds split peas
    1 cup diced ham
    1 gallon water
    $1/3$ cup chicken base
    $1/4$ cup ham base
    2 bay leaves
    $1/2$ teaspoon white pepper
    2 cups heavy cream

Sauté the celery and onions in the butter in a stockpot over medium-high heat until tender. Add the split peas and ham and mix well. Cook for 15 to 20 minutes.

Add the water, chicken base and ham base and mix well. Stir in the bay leaves and white pepper. Cook over low heat for $1^1/2$ to 2 hours or until the peas are tender. Stir in the heavy cream. Cook for 20 minutes. Remove the bay leaves before serving.

Yield: 1 gallon

Curried Pumpkin Soup

3 cups chopped onions
$1/2$ teaspoon garlic powder
1 tablespoon curry powder
$1/2$ cup (1 stick) butter
$1/2$ cup flour
1 gallon water
$1/3$ cup chicken base
1 quart heavy cream
6 cups pumpkin purée
$1/2$ teaspoon white pepper
$1/2$ teaspoon crushed red pepper

Sauté the onions, garlic powder and curry powder in the butter in a stockpot over medium-high heat until the onions are tender. Add the flour. Cook for 10 minutes, stirring constantly.

Add the water, chicken base, heavy cream and pumpkin purée and mix well. Cook for 20 minutes. Stir in the white pepper and crushed red pepper.

Yield: 2 gallons

Restaurateur Shares Success (and the Stove) with Daughters

eghan and Caitlin Murray recently found out why their mother is so tired when she gets home from her restaurants. The girls went to work with their mother, owner/ operator Norma Fleming Murray, as part of the "Take Our Daughters to Work Day." Meghan, age 13, made six asparagus quiches, while 10-year-old Caitlin stirred up chicken pasta soup and cream of celery soup. "My family has always been a big part of my business," says Murray. "Although the girls have spent a lot of time here, they have never spent the entire day with me, and I have never let them cook before." When their cooking duties were completed, Meghan and Caitlin went from the back of the house to the front to greet and seat customers. "Having the girls in the restaurant really added a personal touch to the service for the day."

–Article in June/July 1993 issue of *Restaurants USA* magazine

Most preschool children get up, have breakfast, catch a carpool, and go to school. Not our child. When I began work at the café, Caitlin often came with me until I could drop her off at school.

She would sit in my kitchen as I started the day's soups and breads—drawing on parchment paper I would later bake on! On other days, she would spend her mornings with her dad. As he made rounds at the hospital, she would watch through the glass windows as Dad "checked the babies." How many four-year-olds can tell you about the café's specials and the newborn nursery?

In December 2000, my husband cleaned his car. In his glove compartment, he found a washcloth and a comb. Caitlin recognized these items as ones Dad used to "clean her up" before he dropped her off at school. What a lucky child!

—Norma

Entrées
As Always

Beef Burgundy Stew

4 pounds lean beef, cubed
Flour
$1/2$ cup (1 stick) butter
2 pounds potatoes, diced
2 pounds baby carrots
2 cups coarsely chopped onions
6 slices bacon, chopped
$1/2$ cup beef base
1 quart burgundy wine
4 bay leaves
1 tablespoon garlic powder
$1/2$ tablespoon thyme
2 tablespoons tomato paste
$1/4$ cup brandy
$1/2$ tablespoon black pepper

Coat the beef lightly with flour. Cook in the butter in a skillet over medium-high heat until browned, stirring frequently. Combine the beef, potatoes, carrots, onions, bacon, beef base, burgundy wine, bay leaves, garlic powder, thyme, tomato paste, brandy and black pepper in a baking crock and mix well.

Bake, covered, at 300 degrees for 2 hours or until the vegetables are tender, adding water as needed. Remove the bay leaves before serving.

Yield: $2^1/2$ gallons

Chicken Almondine

1/2 cup chopped onion
1 cup (2 sticks) butter
1/2 cup flour
1 quart milk
1 quart water
1/4 cup chicken base
3 bay leaves
1/2 tablespoon white pepper
4 egg yolks
2 cups half-and-half
1/4 cup dry sherry
5 pounds boneless skinless chicken breasts,
    cooked, chopped
1 cup toasted almonds
Seasoned bread crumbs

Sauté the onion in the butter in a skillet over medium-high heat until light brown. Add the flour. Cook until bubbly, stirring constantly. Add the milk, water and chicken base and whisk until smooth. Stir in the bay leaves and white pepper. Reduce the heat to low.

Combine the egg yolks and half-and-half in a bowl and mix well. Stir in the dry sherry. Add to the warm sauce gradually, whisking continually. Whisk until smooth. Add chicken and almonds and mix well. Spoon into two 8x11-inch baking pans. Sprinkle with seasoned bread crumbs. Bake at 350 degrees for 20 minutes or until bubbly.

Yield: 10 to 12 servings

Chicken and Artichoke Casserole

1/2 cup (1 stick) butter
5 pounds boneless skinless chicken breasts
Salt
Black pepper
Paprika
1 pound mushrooms, thickly sliced
1/3 cup melted butter
4 cans artichoke hearts, drained
1/2 cup (1 stick) butter
1/2 cup flour
1/3 cup chicken base
2 cups water
1/2 cup dry sherry

Place 4 tablespoons butter in each of two baking dishes. Heat in a 375-degree oven until melted.

Sprinkle the chicken with salt, black pepper and paprika. Arrange in the prepared baking dishes, turning to coat with butter. Bake for 15 to 20 minutes. Sauté the mushrooms in butter in a skillet over medium-high heat.

Arrange the mushrooms and artichoke hearts around the chicken in the baking dish. Melt 1/2 cup butter in a skillet. Add the flour and stir until the mixture is smooth. Add the chicken base, water and sherry gradually, stirring constantly. Pour over the chicken and vegetables. Bake for 30 minutes.

Yield: 12 servings

Chicken Dijon

12 boneless skinless chicken breasts
1 cup milk
2 cups sour cream
1 cup Dijon mustard
1 tablespoon paprika
1/2 tablespoon celery salt
2 tablespoons Worcestershire sauce
1 tablespoon lemon juice
1 teaspoon garlic powder
1 teaspoon white pepper
1 cup bread crumbs or cracker crumbs

Combine the chicken and milk in a shallow dish. Chill, covered, for 1 hour. Combine the sour cream, Dijon mustard, paprika, celery salt, Worcestershire sauce, lemon juice, garlic powder and white pepper in a bowl and mix well.

Remove the chicken from the milk and discard the milk. Dip the chicken in the sour cream mixture. Coat with the bread crumbs. Arrange in a baking dish. Bake at 350 degrees for 40 minutes.

Yield: 12 servings

Chicken Divan

5 pounds boneless skinless chicken breasts
Flour
3 cups sour cream
3 cups half-and-half
1/4 cup chicken base
1 teaspoon garlic powder
1 teaspoon white pepper
1/2 cup dry sherry
2 cups mixed shredded Cheddar, Monterey Jack and
    Parmesan cheese
4 cups cooked rice
Broccoli flowerettes, steamed

Coat the chicken lightly with flour. Arrange in a greased shallow baking pan. Bake at 350 degrees for 20 minutes. Combine the sour cream, half-and-half, chicken base, garlic powder, white pepper and dry sherry in a bowl and mix well. Pour over the chicken.

Bake for 20 minutes. Sprinkle with the cheese mixture. Bake for 10 minutes longer. Serve over rice with broccoli.

Yield: 10 to 12 servings

Chicken Enchiladas

6 cups chopped cooked chicken
2 cans cream of chicken soup
2 cups picante sauce
12 flour tortillas
1 cup salsa
2 cups sour cream
1 cup mixed shredded Monterey Jack and Cheddar cheese
Tostada chips

Combine the chicken, soup and picante sauce in a bowl and mix well. Brush the tortillas with the salsa. Spoon 1/2 cup of the chicken mixture onto each tortilla. Roll to enclose the filling.

Arrange seam side down in greased shallow baking pans. Spread with the sour cream. Sprinkle with the cheese mixture. Bake at 350 degrees for 20 to 25 minutes or until bubbly. Serve with tostada chips.

Yield: 8 to 10 servings

Chicken Italiano

5 pounds boneless skinless chicken breasts
1 quart zesty Italian salad dressing
1 quart Marinara Sauce (page 82)
6 cups cooked fettuccini
2 cups freshly grated Parmesan cheese

Arrange the chicken in baking pans. Pour the salad dressing over the chicken. Bake at 350 degrees for 30 minutes. Drain drippings from pans.

Pour the Marinara Sauce over the chicken. Bake for 20 minutes longer. Serve over fettuccini. Sprinkle with the cheese.

Yield: 10 to 12 servings

Chicken Marsala

5 pounds boneless skinless chicken breasts
Flour
$1/2$ gallon brown gravy
1 cup sliced onion
2 cups thickly sliced mushrooms
$1/2$ cup marsala
Chopped fresh parsley
4 cups cooked bow tie pasta

Coat the chicken lightly with flour. Arrange in baking pans. Bake at 350 degrees for 20 minutes. Add brown gravy, onion and mushrooms.

Bake for 20 minutes or until chicken tests done and gravy is bubbly. Stir in the marsala. Let stand for 5 to 10 minutes. Sprinkle with parsley. Serve over bow tie pasta.

Yield: 8 to 10 servings

Chicken and Wild Rice

1 cup chopped onion
1 cup (2 sticks) butter
1/2 cup flour
1/4 cup chicken base
2 cups water
3 cups half-and-half
2 cups wild rice, cooked
1 cup sliced mushrooms
6 cups chopped cooked chicken
1/4 cup chopped fresh parsley
1/2 teaspoon black pepper
1/2 cup slivered almonds

Sauté the onion in the butter in a skillet over medium-high heat until tender but not brown. Remove from the heat. Stir in the flour. Add the chicken base and water gradually, stirring constantly. Add the half-and-half. Cook until the mixture is thickened, stirring constantly.

Stir in the wild rice, mushrooms, chicken, parsley and black pepper. Spoon into a baking dish. Sprinkle with the almonds. Bake at 350 degrees for 30 minutes.

Yield: 12 servings

Creole Jambalaya

4 cups chopped onions
4 cups chopped celery
4 cups chopped green bell pepper
$1/2$ cup olive oil
$1/2$ gallon rice
1 tablespoon Cajun seasoning
$1/2$ tablespoon black pepper
$1/4$ teaspoon red pepper
$1/4$ cup seafood base
$1/4$ cup ham base
1 gallon water
4 cups sliced sausage
3 cups peeled shrimp
1 cup tomato paste

Sauté the onions, celery and bell pepper in the olive oil in a stockpot over medium-high heat until tender.

Add the rice, Cajun seasoning, black pepper, red pepper, seafood base, ham base, water, sausage, shrimp and tomato paste and mix well. Cook for 35 to 40 minutes or until the water is absorbed.

Yield: 1 gallon

Curried Chicken and Broccoli

1 bunch broccoli, broken into flowerettes, steamed
8 boneless skinless chicken breasts
3 cans cream of chicken soup
1$\frac{1}{2}$ cups mayonnaise
1 teaspoon lemon juice
1 teaspoon curry powder
$\frac{1}{2}$ cup shredded Cheddar cheese
$\frac{1}{2}$ cup crushed croutons
1 tablespoon butter, melted

Arrange the broccoli in a baking pan. Arrange the chicken on top of the broccoli. Combine the soup, mayonnaise, lemon juice and curry powder in a bowl and mix well. Pour over the chicken. Sprinkle with the cheese and croutons. Drizzle with the butter. Bake at 350 degrees for 40 minutes.

Yield: 8 servings

Ginger Nut Chicken

5 pounds boneless skinless chicken breasts
$^1/_2$ cup (1 stick) butter, melted
2 cups crushed walnuts
2 cups shredded coconut
1 tablespoon ginger
1 teaspoon garlic powder
1 teaspoon white pepper
Fruit Mustard (page 81)

Coat the chicken with the butter. Combine the walnuts, coconut, ginger, garlic powder and white pepper in a bowl and mix well. Roll the chicken in the walnut mixture. Arrange in greased shallow baking pans. Bake at 350 degrees for 40 minutes or until brown. Serve with Fruit Mustard.

Yield: 8 to 10 servings

Mexicali Chicken

5 pounds boneless skinless chicken breasts
Flour
1 quart mild salsa
1 (12-ounce) can beer
1/4 cup chicken base
1 teaspoon cayenne pepper
Shredded Monterey Jack and Cheddar cheeses
1 cup chopped green bell pepper
1 cup chopped red bell pepper
1/2 cup chopped green onions
1/4 cup (1/2 stick) butter
6 cups hot cooked white rice

Coat the chicken lightly with flour. Arrange in baking pans. Bake at 350 degrees for 25 minutes; drain. Combine the salsa, beer, chicken base and cayenne pepper in a bowl and mix well. Pour over the chicken.

Bake for 20 minutes. Sprinkle with the cheese mixture. Sauté the bell peppers and green onions in the butter in a skillet over medium-high heat until tender. Add the rice and toss to mix well. Serve with the chicken.

Yield: 10 to 12 servings

Orange Chicken

>**5 pounds boneless skinless chicken breasts**
>**$1/2$ cup chopped green onions**
>**1 cup (2 sticks) butter**
>**1 cup flour**
>**4 cups orange juice**
>**$1/4$ cup chicken base**
>**1 cup dry white wine**
>**1 teaspoon white pepper**
>**1 tablespoon tarragon**
>**1 cup sliced black olives**
>**2 cups chopped artichoke hearts**
>**Pasta**

Arrange chicken in greased shallow baking pans. Bake at 350 degrees for 20 minutes; drain. Sauté the green onions in the butter in a skillet over medium-high heat until tender. Add the flour. Cook until light brown.

Add the orange juice, chicken base, white wine, white pepper and tarragon. Cook until thickened and smooth, stirring constantly. Pour over chicken. Add the black olives and artichoke hearts. Bake for 25 minutes or until bubbly. Serve over pasta.

Yield: 8 to 10 servings

Sour Cream Chicken

5 pounds boneless skinless chicken breasts
2 cups sour cream
$1/2$ tablespoon garlic powder
$1/4$ cup Worcestershire sauce
1 tablespoon lemon juice
$1/2$ teaspoon celery seeds
$1/4$ cup chicken base
2 cups crushed seasoned croutons
Wild rice

Arrange the chicken in greased shallow baking pans. Combine the sour cream, garlic powder, Worcestershire sauce, lemon juice, celery seeds and chicken base in a bowl and mix well. Spread over the chicken.

Bake at 350 degrees for 35 to 40 minutes. Sprinkle with the crushed croutons. Bake for 10 minutes longer. Serve over wild rice.

Yield: 10 to 12 servings

Shrimp Florentine

1 cup finely chopped onion
1 cup (2 sticks) butter
3/4 cup flour
1 teaspoon salt
2 teaspoons dry mustard
8 cups milk
1/4 cup seafood base
1 cup shredded Swiss
    cheese
2 cups grated Parmesan
    cheese

1 (40-ounce) package frozen
    chopped spinach, thawed
2 (8-ounce) cans sliced
    water chestnuts
5 pounds shrimp, cooked,
    peeled
1/3 cup lemon juice
1 cup shredded Swiss
    cheese
2 cups grated Parmesan
    cheese

Sauté the onion in the butter in a large skillet over medium-high heat until tender. Stir in the flour, salt and dry mustard. Add the milk and seafood base. Cook until the sauce thickens, stirring constantly. Stir in 1 cup Swiss cheese and 2 cups Parmesan cheese. Remove from the heat.

Combine the spinach and water chestnuts in a bowl and mix well. Spoon into a greased shallow baking pan. Drizzle with the lemon juice. Arrange the shrimp on top of the spinach mixture. Pour the sauce evenly over the shrimp. Sprinkle with a mixture of 1 cup Swiss cheese and 2 cups Parmesan cheese. Bake at 350 degrees for 30 minutes.

Yield: 12 servings

Shrimp with Mushroom Sauce

¹/₄ cup (¹/₂ stick) butter
5 cups shrimp
3 cups sliced mushrooms
3 cups sour cream
1 teaspoon salt
1 tablespoon Worcestershire sauce
2 tablespoons dill weed
1 tablespoon paprika
¹/₃ cup fresh lemon juice
5 cups cooked rice

Melt the butter in a medium skillet over low heat. Add the shrimp and mushrooms. Cook until shrimp are pink and tender, stirring occasionally.

Combine the sour cream, salt, Worcestershire sauce, dill weed and paprika in a bowl and mix well. Pour over the shrimp mixture and mix well. Cook until the mixture comes to a boil, stirring constantly. Spoon into a serving dish. Sprinkle with the lemon juice. Serve over the rice.

Yield: 12 servings

Shrimp and Mushroom Vin Blanc

2 pounds mushrooms, sliced
1 cup sliced green onions
1 cup (2 sticks) butter
1 cup flour
2 cups white wine
1 teaspoon white pepper
1 tablespoon seafood base
5 pounds shrimp, boiled
1/4 cup chopped fresh parsley
Rice

Sauté the mushrooms and green onions in the butter in a large skillet over medium-high heat until tender. Stir in the flour. Cook until light brown, stirring constantly.

Add the white wine, white pepper and seafood base and mix well. Cook until thickened, stirring constantly. Stir in the shrimp and parsley. Serve over rice.

Yield: 8 to 10 servings

Shrimp and Wild Rice Casserole

$1/2$ cup (1 stick) butter, melted
$1/2$ cup flour
2 tablespoons chicken base
1 quart water
2 bay leaves
$1/2$ teaspoon white pepper
$1^1/2$ cups sliced onions
$3/4$ cup sliced green bell pepper
$1^1/2$ cups sliced mushrooms
$3/4$ cup ($1^1/2$ sticks) butter, melted
3 tablespoons Worcestershire sauce
1 tablespoon seafood base
3 or 4 drops of Tabasco sauce
6 cups wild rice, cooked
3 pounds shrimp, cooked, peeled

For the cream sauce, melt $1/2$ cup butter in a saucepan over low heat. Whisk in the flour. Cook for 10 minutes, stirring constantly. Add the chicken base, water, bay leaves and white pepper and mix well. Cook for 15 to 20 minutes, whisking frequently.

For the casserole, sauté the onions, bell pepper and mushrooms in $3/4$ cup butter in a large skillet over medium-high heat until tender. Add the Worcestershire sauce, seafood base, Tabasco sauce, wild rice, shrimp and cream sauce and mix well. Spoon into a baking dish. Bake at 325 degrees for 30 minutes.

Yield: 12 servings

Dill Vegetables and Pasta

4 cups mayonnaise
4 cups sour cream
2 tablespoons dill weed
1 tablespoon seasoned salt
1 teaspoon lemon juice
1 tablespoon chopped onion
8 cups chopped fresh vegetables,
    such as zucchini, squash, mushrooms, carrots, broccoli,
    cauliflower and asparagus
Chopped tomatoes
Pasta

Combine the mayonnaise, sour cream, dill weed, seasoned salt, lemon juice and onion in a blender. Process until smooth. Arrange the vegetables in a greased shallow baking pan.

Bake at 375 degrees for 35 minutes. Spread the mayonnaise mixture over the vegetables. Bake for 10 to 15 minutes or until bubbly. Top with chopped tomatoes. Serve over pasta or serve as a side dish.

Yield: 8 to 10 servings

Chicken and Broccoli Crepes

4 cups chopped cooked chicken
4 cups chopped steamed broccoli
Mornay Sauce (page 79)
24 crepe shells
Shredded Swiss cheese

Combine the chicken and broccoli in a bowl and mix well. Add enough of the Mornay Sauce to bind the ingredients together. Spoon $1/2$ cup chicken mixture onto each crepe shell. Arrange in lightly greased baking dishes. Spoon remaining Mornay Sauce over the crepes. Bake at 350 degrees for 15 to 20 minutes. Sprinkle with Swiss cheese.

Yield: 24 servings

For Ham and Asparagus Crepes, substitute finely chopped cooked ham and finely chopped steamed asparagus for the chicken and broccoli.

For Shrimp and Mushroom Crepes, omit the chicken and broccoli and sauté 4 cups partially cooked shrimp and 4 cups sliced mushrooms in 1 cup white wine until tender; drain. Proceed as recipe directs.

For Primavera Crepes, substitute 8 cups lightly steamed chopped fresh vegetables and 1 cup freshly grated Parmesan cheese for the chicken and broccoli.

Mornay Sauce

1 cup (2 sticks) butter, melted
1 cup flour
$1/2$ gallon milk
$1/4$ teaspoon white pepper
$1/4$ teaspoon garlic powder
2 bay leaves
1 cup grated Parmesan cheese
1 cup shredded Swiss cheese

Melt the butter in a large saucepan over low heat. Stir in the flour. Add the milk, white pepper, garlic powder and bay leaves. Cook until smooth, stirring constantly. Stir in Parmesan cheese and Swiss cheese. Cook until thickened, stirring constantly. Remove the bay leaves before serving.

Yield: (about) 2 quarts

Red Beans

1 pound onions, chopped
3/4 pound celery, chopped
1/2 pound green bell peppers, chopped
1/2 cup bacon drippings
1/2 cup (1 stick) margarine
1/2 pound ham, chopped
1 pound sausage, sliced

$1^1/_2$ pounds dried red kidney beans
1/3 cup ham base
1 tablespoon garlic powder
1/4 teaspoon black pepper
1/4 teaspoon cayenne pepper
2 bay leaves

Sauté the onions, celery and bell peppers in the bacon drippings and margarine in a large saucepan over medium-high heat until tender. Add the ham, sausage and kidney beans and mix well. Cook for 30 minutes, stirring occasionally.

Add the ham base, garlic powder, black pepper, cayenne pepper, bay leaves and enough water to cover and mix well. Cook over low heat until beans are tender, adding additional water if needed.

Yield: 1 gallon

Every mom has a smell. That certain scent that is instantly recognizable to her kids. My mom had a smell, but it definitely was not like other mothers. Every day when my mom would pick me up from preschool, I would run and give her a big hug. And then I would sniff. "Jambalaya." "Red Beans." "Gumbo." It was my game, every afternoon, to figure out what my mom had cooked that day in the café by sniffing her when I gave her a hug. And I always hit it right on the nose!

—Caitlin

Fruit Mustard

**1 (12-ounce) jar apricot or
red raspberry preserves
1/2 cup (1 stick) butter, melted
1 cup Grey Poupon mustard
1/4 cup white wine, optional**

Combine the preserves, butter, mustard and white wine in a blender. Process until blended.

Use as a dip for chicken tenders or spread over partially baked chicken breasts and continue baking until chicken is cooked through.

Yield: 3 cups

Marinara Sauce

4 cups chopped onions
2 cups chopped green bell peppers
$^1/_4$ cup olive oil
4 large cans crushed tomatoes
1 large can tomato sauce
4 bay leaves
2 tablespoons basil
1 tablespoon thyme
$^1/_2$ tablespoon garlic powder
$^1/_2$ tablespoon sugar

Sauté the onions and bell peppers in the olive oil in a large saucepan over medium-high heat until tender. Add the crushed tomatoes and tomato sauce. Reduce the heat to low. Cook for 30 minutes, stirring frequently. Add the bay leaves, basil, thyme, garlic powder and sugar and mix well. Cook for 1 hour, stirring occasionally. Serve over pasta.

May add cooked meat, seafood base or burgundy or merlot wine.

Yield: 1$^1/_2$ gallons

 How do you know you've made someone mad in a commercial kitchen? In my case, my work shoes, which I left tucked under my work table at the end of each day, were filled with olive oil—what a mess! No marinara sauce that day!

I have always been proud of my mom and what she's accomplished, and I've grown accustomed to people's surprised and thrilled reactions when they learn I'm "Norma's daughter." Only once in my life has this relationship been questioned.

When I was eight years old, I was a dancing "bon-bon" in The Nutcracker. One evening while we were waiting for our turn on stage, the other girls and I began to talk about what our moms did. I was completely unprepared to defend my title as "Norma's daughter," but another "bon-bon" insisted that I was lying and that I was not Norma's daughter.

Well, I was determined to prove myself by whatever means necessary; I brought back the all-powerful parent note. I told my mom what happened and she gave me a special note on her authentic Norma's stationery: "To Candace: My biggest fan! Norma." The note did the trick, and I've never had to prove I'm "Norma's daughter" since.

–Caitlin

83

Growing up with a mom who ran restaurants, I never gave much consideration to the enormous demands she faced. In my eyes, it was always simply "what she does." It is only within the last few years that the accomplishments of my mother have truly taken on a more significant meaning for me. As a college graduate about to embark on a career of my own, I am beginning to understand just how much my mother has accomplished in fourteen years. I read the statistics that only one in ten restaurants survives its first year, with an even lower success rate for restaurants owned by women. I see the compromises all women must make to fulfill both career goals and family obligations. I wonder if I'll ever be able to accomplish as much as my mom already has. I've come to realize that, while the restaurants may be "just" what my mom does, it is the flair and perseverance with which she has done it, the challenges she has overcome, and the success story she has written that will continue to impress me and make me proud for the rest of my life.

—Meghan

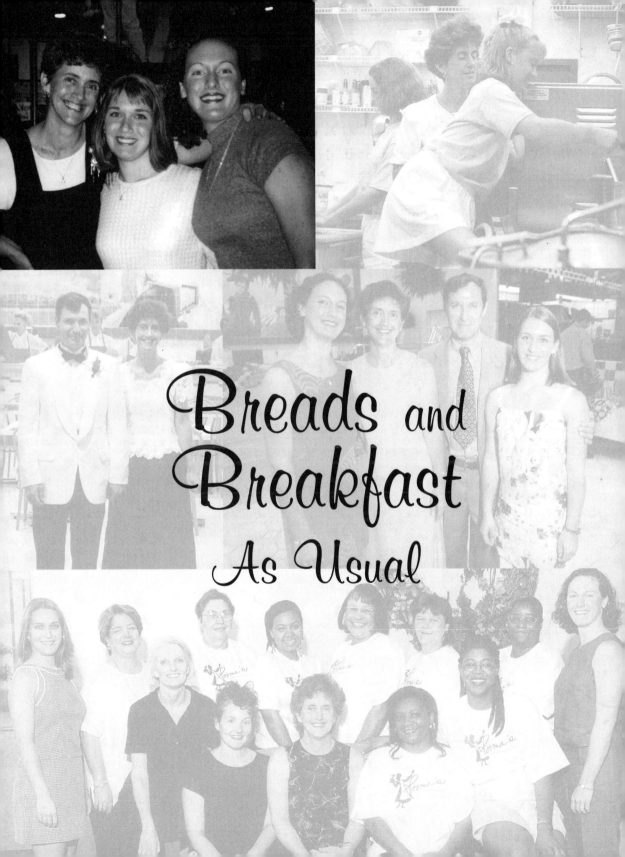

Breads and Breakfast
As Usual

Norma's Poppy Seed Bread

2 cups sugar
1¹/₂ cups vegetable oil
4 eggs
1 (13-ounce) can evaporated milk
1 teaspoon vanilla extract
4 cups flour
1¹/₂ tablespoons baking powder
1 teaspoon salt
1 cup poppy seeds

Combine the sugar, oil, eggs, evaporated milk and vanilla in a mixing bowl and beat until smooth. Sift the flour, baking powder and salt together.

Add to the sugar mixture and mix well. Add the poppy seeds and mix well. Spoon into 2 greased loaf pans. Bake at 325 degrees for 40 to 45 minutes.

Yield: 2 loaves

Apple Nut Bread

1 cup (2 sticks) margarine, softened
1½ cups packed brown sugar
4 eggs
4 cups flour
¼ teaspoon salt
2 teaspoons baking soda
3 cups apple pie filling
1 cup chopped pecans or walnuts

Combine the margarine and brown sugar in a mixing bowl. Beat until creamy.
Add the eggs and mix well.

Combine the flour, salt and baking soda. Beat into the margarine mixture. Stir in
apple pie filling and pecans. Spoon into 2 greased and floured loaf pans. Bake at
300 degrees for 45 to 50 minutes.

Yield: 2 loaves

Apricot Braid

6 cups (about) flour
3/4 cup sugar
1 teaspoon salt
3 envelopes dry yeast
1/2 cup (1 stick) margarine, softened
1 cup warm water (120 to 130 degrees)
3 eggs
2 (18-ounce) jars apricot preserves
1/2 cup packed brown sugar
1 cup finely chopped walnuts
1/2 cup flour
3 tablespoons sugar
3/4 teaspoon cinnamon
3 tablespoons softened margarine

For the dough, combine 1 1/2 cups of the flour, 3/4 cup sugar, the salt and yeast in a mixing bowl and mix well. Add 1/2 cup margarine and the warm water and beat until well mixed.

Add the eggs and 1/2 cup of the flour. Beat at high speed for 2 minutes. Add enough of the remaining 6 cups flour to a make a stiff dough. Knead on a lightly floured surface until smooth and elastic. Divide dough into 3 equal portions. Roll each portion into a 7×12-inch rectangle. Transfer the rectangles to greased baking sheets.

For the filling, combine the preserves, brown sugar and walnuts in a bowl and mix well. Spread one-third of the mixture lengthwise down the center third of each rectangle. Cut 1-inch-wide strips along both sides of the filling, cutting from filling to edges of the dough. Fold the strips at an angle across the filling, alternating from side to side.

Apricot Braid (continued)

For the topping, combine $1/2$ cup flour, 3 tablespoons sugar, cinnamon and 3 tablespoons margarine in a bowl and mix until crumbly. Sprinkle one-third of the mixture on top of each braid. Cover tightly with plastic wrap and freeze until firm.

Remove from baking sheets. Wrap each braid with plastic wrap, then with aluminum foil. Freeze for up to 4 weeks.

Remove from the freezer. Unwrap and place on ungreased baking sheets. Let stand, loosely covered with plastic wrap, for 2 hours or until thawed. Let rise in a warm draft-free place for $1^1/2$ hours or until doubled in bulk.

Bake at 350 degrees for 20 to 25 minutes or until golden. Transfer to wire racks to cool.

Yield: 3 coffee cakes

Cheddar Cheese Bread

7 cups (about) flour
$1/3$ cup sugar
1 tablespoon salt
2 envelopes dry yeast
2 cups water
$2/3$ cup milk
3 cups shredded sharp Cheddar cheese

Combine $2^1/2$ cups of the flour, sugar, salt and yeast in a mixing bowl and mix well. Combine the water and milk in a small saucepan. Cook over medium-low heat until the mixture reaches 120 to 130 degrees, stirring constantly. Add to the flour mixture gradually, beating constantly at medium speed.

Add the cheese and $1/2$ cup flour and beat until well blended. Stir in enough of the remaining flour to make a stiff dough. Knead on a lightly floured surface until smooth and elastic. Place in a greased bowl, turning to coat the surface. Cover with plastic wrap. Let rise in a draft-free place until doubled in bulk.

Punch the dough down. Divide into 2 equal portions. Shape each portion into a 7-inch ball. Place in greased cake pans. Let rise, covered with plastic wrap, until doubled in bulk. Bake at 350 degrees for 35 to 40 minutes. Transfer to wire racks to cool.

Yield: 2 loaves

Cranberry Bread

2 cups flour
1 cup sugar
1¹/₂ teaspoons baking powder
1 teaspoon salt
¹/₂ teaspoon baking soda
¹/₄ cup (¹/₂ stick) margarine
2 eggs, beaten
1 teaspoon orange zest
³/₄ cup orange juice
2 cups cranberries

Combine the flour, sugar, baking powder, salt and baking soda in a bowl and mix well. Cut in the margarine until the mixture is crumbly.

Add the eggs, orange zest and orange juice and mix just until moistened. Fold in the cranberries. Spoon into a greased loaf pan. Bake at 350 degrees for 70 minutes.

Yield: 1 loaf

French Bread

6 cups (about) flour
2 envelopes dry yeast
1 tablespoon sugar
2 teaspoons salt
2 tablespoons shortening
2$^1/_4$ cups warm water (120 to 130 degrees)
1 to 2 tablespoons vegetable oil

Combine 2 cups of the flour, the yeast, sugar and salt in a large mixing bowl and mix well. Add the shortening and warm water. Beat at medium speed for 3 to 4 minutes. Add 1 cup flour and beat at high speed until well blended. Add enough of the remaining flour to make a soft dough. Knead on a floured surface until smooth and elastic. Place in a bowl. Cover with plastic wrap, then a tea towel. Let rise until doubled in bulk.

Punch the dough down. Divide the dough into 2 portions. Roll each portion into an 8×15-inch rectangle. Roll as for a jelly roll, beginning at 1 long side; seal the seams. Place seam side down on greased baking sheets. Brush lightly with oil. Cover loosely with plastic wrap. Chill until doubled in bulk. Brush loaves with cold water.

Bake at 375 degrees for 35 to 40 minutes; bread will sound hollow when tapped. Let bread stand in oven for 5 to 10 minutes. Transfer loaves to wire racks to cool.

Yield: 2 loaves

Lemon Bread

4 cups flour
2 cups sugar
1¹/₂ tablespoons baking powder
1 teaspoon salt
2 cups (4 sticks) butter, melted
1 cup lemon juice
8 eggs, separated

Combine the flour, sugar, baking powder and salt in a bowl and mix well. Cut in the butter with a pastry blender. Beat in the lemon juice. Add the egg yolks and mix well.

Beat the egg whites in a mixing bowl until stiff peaks form. Add to the butter mixture and mix well. Spoon into 2 greased loaf pans. Bake at 325 degrees for 45 minutes.

Yield: 2 loaves

Pumpkin Bread

1 1/2 cups flour
1 cup sugar
1/2 teaspoon salt
1 teaspoon baking soda
1 cup pumpkin purée
1/2 cup chopped pineapple, drained
1/2 cup vegetable oil
2 eggs, beaten
1/4 cup water
1/4 teaspoon nutmeg
1/4 teaspoon cinnamon
1/4 teaspoon allspice
1/2 cup chopped nuts

Sift the flour, sugar, salt and baking soda into a bowl. Combine the pumpkin, pineapple, oil, eggs, water, nutmeg, cinnamon and allspice in a bowl and mix well. Add to the flour mixture and mix just until moistened. Stir in the nuts. Spoon into a greased loaf pan.

Bake at 350 degrees for 50 to 60 minutes or until a straw inserted in the center comes out clean. Transfer loaf to a wire rack to cool.

Yield: 1 loaf

Rye Bread

4 cups all-purpose flour
2 cups rye flour
1¹/₂ teaspoons salt
1 tablespoon caraway seeds
2 envelopes dry yeast
¹/₄ cup (¹/₂ stick) butter, softened
2 cups warm water (120 to 130 degrees)
¹/₃ cup molasses

Combine the all-purpose flour and rye flour in a large bowl and mix well. Combine 2 cups of the flour mixture, salt, caraway seeds and yeast in a mixing bowl and mix well. Add the butter and mix well. Add the water and molasses. Beat at medium speed for 3 to 4 minutes. Add 1 cup of the flour mixture and beat at high speed for 3 to 4 minutes. Stir in enough of the remaining flour mixture to make a stiff dough.

Knead on a floured surface until smooth and elastic. Cover with plastic wrap, then a tea towel. Let rise in a warm draft-free place for 1 hour or until doubled in bulk.

Punch the dough down. Divide into 2 portions. Shape each portion into a 7-inch round loaf. Place in greased cake pans. Let rise until doubled in bulk. Bake at 350 degrees for 35 to 40 minutes; bread will sound hollow when tapped. Transfer loaves to wire racks to cool.

May shape dough into loaves and place in greased loaf pans.

Yield: 2 loaves

Sourdough White Bread

3¹/₂ cups flour
1 tablespoon sugar
1 envelope dry yeast
2 cups warm water (120 to 130 degrees)
2 cups flour
1 envelope dry yeast
3 tablespoons sugar
1 teaspoon salt
³/₄ cup milk
¹/₄ cup water
2 tablespoons margarine
3 cups flour

For the sourdough starter, combine 3¹/₂ cups flour, 1 tablespoon sugar and
1 envelope yeast in a large bowl and mix well. Add the warm water gradually,
beating constantly. Beat until smooth. Cover with plastic wrap. Let stand in
a warm place for 3 days.

For the bread, combine 2 cups flour, 1 envelope yeast, 3 tablespoons sugar
and salt in a bowl and mix well. Combine the milk, ¹/₄ cup water and margarine
in a saucepan.

Cook over medium-low heat until the temperature reaches 120 to 130 degrees,
stirring constantly. Add the milk mixture to the flour mixture. Beat at medium
speed until well mixed. Add 1¹/₂ cups starter and 1 cup of the remaining flour
and beat until smooth. Stir in enough of the remaining flour to make a
stiff dough.

Sourdough White Bread (continued)

Knead on a lightly floured surface until smooth and elastic. Place in a greased bowl, turning to coat the surface. Cover with plastic wrap. Let rise in a warm, draft-free place until doubled in bulk.

Punch the dough down. Divide into 2 equal portions. Shape each portion into a 14-inch-long loaf or a 7-inch ball. Place on greased baking sheets or in greased cake pans.

Make several diagonal cuts on the tops of the long loaves or make several crisscross cuts on the tops of the round loaves. Cover with plastic wrap. Chill long loaves until doubled in bulk or let round loaves rise in a warm draft-free place until doubled in bulk. Bake at 375 degrees for 25 to 30 minutes. Transfer loaves to wire racks to cool.

Yield: 2 loaves

Tricolor Braid Bread

3 1/2 cups all-purpose flour
2 envelopes dry yeast
1 tablespoon salt
2 1/2 cups water
2 tablespoons honey
1/4 cup (1/2 stick) margarine
1 1/2 cups all-purpose flour
2 tablespoons honey
2 tablespoons wheat germ
1 1/2 cups whole wheat flour
2 tablespoons dark molasses
2 tablespoons baking cocoa
1 1/2 teaspoons caraway seeds
1 1/2 cups rye flour
1 egg yolk

Combine the all-purpose flour, yeast and salt in a bowl and mix well. Combine the water, 2 tablespoons honey and margarine in a saucepan. Cook over medium-low heat until the temperature reaches 120 to 130 degrees, stirring constantly. Add to the flour mixture and beat well.

Divide batter into 3 equal portions in bowls. For the white bread, add 1 1/2 cups all-purpose flour to 1 portion of batter and mix well. Knead on a lightly floured surface until smooth and elastic. Place in a greased bowl, turning to coat the surface. Let rise, covered, in a warm draft-free place until doubled in bulk.

For the whole wheat bread, add 2 tablespoons honey, wheat germ and whole wheat flour to 1 portion of batter and mix well. Knead on a lightly floured surface until smooth and elastic. Place in a greased bowl, turning to coat the surface. Let rise, covered, in a warm draft-free place until doubled in bulk.

Tricolor Braid Bread (continued)

For the pumpernickel bread, add molasses, cocoa, caraway seeds and rye flour and mix well. Knead on a lightly floured surface until smooth and elastic. Place in a greased bowl, turning to coat the surface.

Let rise, covered, in a warm draft-free place until doubled in bulk. Punch each portion of the dough down. Divide each portion into halves. Shape each portion into a smooth 15-inch rope.

For each loaf, place 1 white, 1 whole wheat and 1 pumpernickel rope on a greased baking sheet. Braid loosely and pinch ends to seal, tucking ends under. Let rise, loosely covered, in a warm place for $1^1/_2$ hours or until doubled in bulk.

Combine the egg yolk with a small amount of water in a bowl. Brush loaves with the egg yolk mixture. Bake at 350 degrees for 35 minutes or until browned. Transfer loaves to wire racks to cool.

Yield: 2 loaves

Whole Wheat Bread

4$\frac{1}{2}$ cups all-purpose flour
2$\frac{1}{2}$ cups whole wheat flour
1 cup wheat germ
$\frac{1}{3}$ cup sugar
1 tablespoon salt
2 envelopes dry yeast
2 cups milk
$\frac{3}{4}$ cup water
$\frac{1}{4}$ cup ($\frac{1}{2}$ stick) margarine
$\frac{1}{3}$ cup honey

Combine the all-purpose flour, whole wheat flour and wheat germ in a bowl and mix well. Combine 3 cups of the flour mixture, the sugar, salt and yeast in a bowl and mix well.

Combine the milk, water, margarine and honey in a saucepan. Cook over medium-low heat until the temperature reaches 120 to 130 degrees, stirring constantly. Add to the flour mixture. Beat at medium speed until well mixed. Add 1 cup of the flour mixture. Beat at high speed until well blended. Stir in enough of the remaining flour mixture to make a stiff dough.

Knead on a lightly floured surface until smooth and elastic. Place in a greased bowl, turning to coat the surface. Cover with plastic wrap, then a tea towel. Let rise in a warm draft-free place until doubled in bulk. Punch the dough down.

Divide into 2 equal portions. Shape each portion into a loaf. Place in greased loaf pans. Let rise, covered with plastic wrap, until the dough reaches the tops of the pans. Bake at 350 degrees for 35 minutes; bread will sound hollow when tapped. Transfer loaves to wire racks to cool.

Yield: 2 loaves

Mama Muffins

2 cups flour
$3/4$ cup sugar
1 tablespoon baking powder
$1/2$ teaspoon salt
1 cup milk
1 egg, beaten
$1/4$ cup ($1/2$ stick) margarine, melted
1 cup chopped fresh fruit (optional)

Combine the flour, sugar, baking powder and salt in a bowl and mix well. Combine the milk, egg and margarine in a bowl and mix well. Add to the flour mixture and mix well. Fold in the fruit. Spoon into lightly greased muffin cups. Bake at 375 degrees for 15 to 20 minutes.

Yield: 12 muffins

For Applesauce Muffins, decrease amount of milk to $1/2$ cup and add $3/4$ cup applesauce to the batter. Brush baked muffins with melted margarine and sprinkle with cinnamon-sugar.

 Mama Muffins are guaranteed to inspire confidence, raise test scores, and ensure general well-being!

Oven French Toast

4 eggs
$2/3$ cup frozen orange juice concentrate, thawed
$1/3$ cup milk
$3/4$ cup sugar
$1/2$ teaspoon vanilla extract
$1/4$ teaspoon nutmeg
$1/4$ teaspoon cinnamon
8 ($1/2$-inch) slices French bread
$1/4$ cup ($1/2$ stick) margarine, melted
$1/2$ cup (1 stick) margarine
$1/2$ cup sugar
$1/2$ cup orange juice

Combine the eggs, orange juice concentrate, milk, $3/4$ cup sugar, vanilla, nutmeg and cinnamon in a bowl and mix well. Grease a 9×13-inch baking pan lightly. Arrange bread in the prepared pan.

Pour the egg mixture evenly over the bread. Chill, covered, for 8 to 12 hours. Let stand at room temperature for 30 to 45 minutes. Drizzle with the melted margarine.

Bake at 350 degrees for 30 minutes or until light brown. Combine $1/2$ cup margarine, $1/2$ cup sugar and the orange juice in a microwave-safe bowl.

Microwave until bubbly, stirring occasionally. Serve over the French toast.

Yield: 6 servings

Piquant Cheese Loaf

6½ cups (about) flour
1 teaspoon sugar
1 tablespoon salt
2 envelopes dry yeast
1 cup plain yogurt
½ cup water
2 tablespoons margarine
6 eggs
8 ounces Muenster cheese, shredded
1 cup sliced boiled ham, julienned
1 egg
1 tablespoon milk

Combine 1½ cups of the flour, sugar, salt and yeast in a mixing bowl and mix well. Combine the yogurt, water and margarine in a saucepan. Cook over medium-low heat until the temperature reaches 120 to 130 degrees, stirring constantly. Add to the flour mixture gradually, beating constantly. Beat until well blended. Add 6 eggs and 1 cup of the flour and mix well. Reserve ½ cup Muenster cheese. Add remaining cheese to the flour mixture. Beat at high speed for 2 to 3 minutes. Stir in enough of the remaining flour to make a stiff dough.

Knead on a lightly floured surface until smooth and elastic. Place in a greased bowl, turning to coat the surface. Let rise, covered, in a warm draft-free place until doubled in bulk. Punch the dough down.

Divide into 2 equal portions. Knead ½ cup ham into each portion. Shape into balls. Place in greased cake pans. Let rise, covered with plastic wrap, until doubled in bulk. Beat the egg in a bowl. Add the milk and mix well. Brush over the loaves. Sprinkle with the remaining Muenster cheese. Bake at 350 degrees for 30 minutes or until golden brown. Transfer loaves to wire racks to cool.

Yield: 2 loaves

Crustless Quiches

1/2 cup shredded Cheddar cheese
1/2 cup shredded mozzarella cheese
1/2 cup shredded Swiss cheese
1/2 cup grated Parmesan cheese
16 eggs
6 cups heavy cream
1 teaspoon basil
1 teaspoon thyme
1 teaspoon white pepper
1/4 cup flour

Spray 2 bundt pans with nonstick cooking spray. Combine the Cheddar cheese, mozzarella cheese, Swiss cheese and Parmesan cheese in a bowl and mix well. Sprinkle on the bottom of the prepared pans.

Combine the eggs, cream, basil, thyme, white pepper and flour in a food processor. Process until well blended. Pour evenly over the cheeses.

Bake at 325 degrees until set and brown. Invert quiches onto a serving platter. Garnish with additional cheese and vegetables.

Yield: 12 to 16 servings

Ham and Cheese Strata

3 cups diced French bread
3 cups diced ham
1 cup shredded Cheddar cheese
1 cup shredded mozzarella cheese
8 eggs
3 cups milk
1 tablespoon dry mustard
1/4 cup flour

Grease a 9×13-inch baking pan. Layer the French bread, ham, Cheddar cheese and mozzarella cheese in the prepared pan. Combine the eggs, milk, dry mustard and flour in a mixing bowl. Beat until frothy. Pour evenly over the layers. Cover with parchment paper and foil. Chill for 8 to 12 hours.

Bake, covered, at 325 degrees for 30 to 35 minutes. Bake, uncovered, for 10 minutes longer or until set.

Yield: 8 to 10 servings

Sausage Pinwheels

2¹/₄ cups baking mix
²/₃ cup milk
1 pound bulk pork sausage

Combine the baking mix and milk in a bowl and mix well. Knead 10 times on a surface sprinkled with baking mix. Roll dough into a ¹/₂-inch-thick rectangle. Spread uncooked sausage over the dough. Roll as for a jelly roll. Cut into ¹/₂-inch slices. Arrange on a baking sheet.

Bake at 350 degrees for 10 to 15 minutes or until the sausage is cooked through.

Yield: 14 to 16 pinwheels

For Ham Pinwheels, spread 2 tablespoons Grey Poupon mustard over the dough. Layer with 8 ounces thinly sliced ham, 4 ounces sliced American cheese and 4 ounces sliced Swiss cheese. Roll as for a jelly roll. Cut into ¹/₂-inch slices. Arrange on a baking sheet. Bake at 350 degrees for 10 minutes or until brown.

Quiche

1 unbaked (9-inch) pie shell
Prepared mustard
1 cup shredded cheese
Chopped fresh vegetables and/or chopped cooked meat
4 eggs
2 cups heavy cream
$1/4$ teaspoon basil
$1/4$ teaspoon thyme
$1/4$ teaspoon white pepper

Brush the pie shell with the mustard. Bake at 350 degrees for 10 minutes. Layer with the cheese, vegetables and/or meat. Combine the eggs, cream, basil, thyme and white pepper in a food processor. Process until well blended. Pour over the layers. Bake at 375 degrees for 25 to 30 minutes or until set.

Yield: 6 to 8 servings

Sausage Bake

1 (8-count) can crescent rolls
1 tablespoon Grey Poupon mustard
$1/2$ cup shredded Cheddar cheese
$1/2$ cup shredded mozzarella cheese
1 pound bulk pork sausage, cooked, crumbled
8 eggs
2 cups milk
$1/4$ cup shredded Cheddar cheese
$1/4$ cup shredded mozzarella cheese

Grease an 8×11-inch baking pan lightly. Line the prepared pan with the crescent roll dough. Brush the dough with the mustard. Bake at 350 degrees for 10 minutes. Layer with $1/2$ cup Cheddar cheese, $1/2$ cup mozzarella cheese and the sausage.

Combine the eggs and milk in a mixing bowl. Beat until frothy. Pour evenly over the sausage. Sprinkle with $1/4$ cup Cheddar cheese and $1/4$ cup mozzarella cheese. Bake at 350 degrees for 35 to 40 minutes or until set.

Yield: 8 servings

Vegetable Soufflé

4 tomato basil bagels, broken into small pieces
1 cup shredded salsa Jack cheese
6 eggs
2 cups milk
1 cup salsa
1 tablespoon dry mustard
1 cup chopped tomatoes
$1/2$ cup shredded Monterey Jack cheese

Grease an 8×11-inch baking pan lightly. Place the bagels in the prepared pan. Sprinkle with the salsa Jack cheese. Combine the eggs, milk, salsa and dry mustard in a bowl and mix well. Pour evenly over the salsa Jack cheese.

Sprinkle with the tomatoes and Monterey Jack cheese. Bake at 325 degrees for 35 to 40 minutes or until set.

Yield: 8 servings

Beignets

5¹/₂ cups (about) flour
¹/₄ cup sugar
1 teaspoon salt
2 envelopes dry yeast
1 cup milk
¹/₄ cup water
¹/₂ cup (1 stick) margarine
3 eggs
Vegetable oil for deep-frying
Confectioners' sugar

Combine 1¹/₂ cups of the flour, the sugar, salt and yeast in a mixing bowl and mix well. Combine the milk, water and margarine in a saucepan. Cook over medium-low heat until the temperature reaches 120 to 130 degrees, stirring constantly. Add gradually to the flour mixture, beating constantly. Beat until well mixed.

Add the eggs and ¹/₂ cup flour. Beat at high speed for 2 minutes. Add enough of the remaining flour to make a stiff dough.

Knead on a lightly floured surface until smooth and elastic. Divide the dough into two equal portions.

Beignets (continued)

Roll each portion into a 9-inch square. Cut each square into nine 3-inch squares. Cut each 3-inch square diagonally into halves. Arrange on greased baking sheets. Cover with plastic wrap. Freeze until firm.

Transfer frozen triangles to a sealable plastic bag. Freeze for up to 5 weeks. Arrange triangles on baking sheets. Cover with plastic wrap. Let stand at room temperature for 1 hour to thaw. Let rise in a warm place until doubled in bulk.

Deep-fry in 375- to 400-degree oil in a deep fryer until golden brown on both sides. Drain on paper towels. Place confectioners' sugar in a clean paper bag. Add beignets and shake to coat.

Yield: 36 beignets

Fresh Fruit Cobbler

3/4 cup flour
3/4 cup sugar
2 teaspoons baking powder
3/4 cup milk
1/4 cup (1/2 stick) margarine
2 cups chopped fresh fruit

Combine the flour, sugar and baking powder in a bowl and mix well. Add the milk and mix until smooth.

Place the margarine in a 9-inch pie plate. Heat in a 350-degree oven until melted. Spoon the flour mixture into the prepared pie plate. Arrange the fruit evenly on top of the batter. Bake at 350 degrees for 25 minutes or until brown.

Yield: 4 servings

When the Boss is a Ma'am—
Norma Fleming Murray

During the past eleven years, Norma Fleming Murray has built what is recognized as one of Pensacola's most unique and successful chains of eating establishments. Looking back, she says her success has been due to many factors, including hard work, taking advantage of opportunities, family support, and a desire to provide her customers the best. She admits, however, that her own early lack of knowledge of the odds played a part, also.

"I didn't know the odds, so I didn't expect to fail," she said, with a smile and a shrug—Murray's reputation as a gourmet cook and clever businesswoman is only exceeded by her reputation as a great boss. Several of the twenty-five employees on her payroll have been with her since she began, a rare longevity in the food service industry. Her explanation for this kind of loyalty is simple.

"I believe it's because I treat them the way that I want to be treated," she said. She also encourages them to be creative, to try new approaches, and not to feel intimidated if they want to test their ideas. "And," she says, "if they need time off for family-related matters, I make allowances." Clearly, being with family has always been a high priority for Murray, and is the main reason her target audience has always been the lunchtime crowd. Her daughters, Meghan, 17, and Caitlin, 14, can often be seen working with their mother in one of the restaurants.

—Excerpted from *Gulf Coast Women's News*
By Rita Shaw Rone
March 13, 1997

Through the years I've made a lot, but poppy seed bread will never stop. One loaf, two loaves, ten and more, customers order it like never before.

Many years have passed at Norma's Café and I have been here since the very first day. So when I think about bread, the poppy seeds stand out—you see, at first we made loaves in small amounts.

But one day Norma had a surprise. The mixer she bought was as big as the sky! The small amount days were over and done. Thirty at once! Yes, Sharon's the one!

I make it at work and think about it at home. Poppy seed bread goes on and on!

I've learned a lot at Norma's Café. I feel like a fixture and will continue to stay. So if you want poppy seed bread, call and we'll make it, but give good notice because I have to bake it!

—Sharon

Desserts
Always Do

Norma's Bread Pudding

3½ cups sugar
1 quart milk
1 quart water
12 eggs, beaten
1 teaspoon salt
1 tablespoon vanilla extract
¾ cup shredded unsweetened coconut
½ cup (1 stick) margarine, melted
6 to 8 cups French bread cubes
Flavored Sauce (page 117)

Combine the sugar, milk and water in a bowl and mix well. Add the eggs, salt, vanilla, coconut and margarine and mix well. Stir in the bread cubes. Let stand until the liquid is absorbed. Spoon into two 9x12-inch baking pans.

Bake at 350 degrees for 35 to 40 minutes or until pudding rises like a soufflé and springs back when touched. Serve with Flavored Sauce.

Yield: 18 to 20 servings

For thirteen years, my dad, Doug Fleming, helped me prepare for the Junior League Marketbasket each November. Since we required gallons and gallons of bread pudding to meet our Marketbasket obligations, my dad would sit out at the beach and "chop" precise squares of bread, bag them in clear garbage bags, and haul them into the café. Dad laughed a lot about this annual job and told me he needed a GINSU knife to do it right. In August 2001, my dad died. As I cleared the condominium, I came across a set of GINSU knives. My dad had truly ordered these knives to do the job well! Amidst the tears, I laughed and thought how lucky I was to have my dad as long as I did. I will miss him always—but most especially at Marketbasket time.

Flavored Sauce

4 whole eggs, or $1/2$ cup egg substitute
$1/4$ cup whiskey, lemon juice or amaretto
2 cups confectioners' sugar
1 cup (2 sticks) margarine, melted

Combine the eggs and flavoring (whiskey, lemon juice or amaretto) in a food processor. Process until well blended. Add the confectioners' sugar and margarine and process until smooth.

Yield: 1 quart

Apple Bread Pudding

3¹/₂ cups sugar
1 quart milk
1 quart water
12 eggs, beaten
1 teaspoon salt
1 tablespoon vanilla extract
1 tablespoon cinnamon
1 teaspoon nutmeg
¹/₂ cup (1 stick) margarine, melted
6 to 8 cups French bread cubes
3 cups chopped apples
1 cup chopped pecans
Brown Sauce (page 119)

Combine the sugar, milk and water in a bowl and mix well. Add the eggs, salt, vanilla, cinnamon, nutmeg and margarine and mix well. Stir in the bread cubes, apples and pecans. Let stand until the liquid is absorbed. Spoon into two 9x12-inch baking pans.

Bake at 350 degrees for 35 to 40 minutes. Serve with the Brown Sauce.

Yield: 18 to 20 servings

Brown Sauce

4 whole eggs, or $1/2$ cup egg substitute
$1/4$ cup cinnamon schnapps or apple brandy
2 cups packed dark brown sugar
1 cup (2 sticks) margarine, melted

Combine the eggs and flavoring in a food processor. Process until well blended. Add the brown sugar and margarine. Process until smooth.

Yield: 1 quart

Fiesta Bread Pudding

3 cups sugar
1 quart milk
1 quart water
12 eggs, beaten
1 teaspoon salt
1 tablespoon vanilla extract
1 tablespoon orange flavoring
$1/2$ cup (1 stick) margarine, melted
6 to 8 cups Cuban bread cubes
2 large cans fruit cocktail, drained
Orange Sauce (page 121)

Combine the sugar, milk and water in a bowl and mix well. Add the eggs, salt, vanilla, orange flavoring and margarine and mix well. Stir in the bread cubes and fruit cocktail. Let stand until the liquid is absorbed. Spoon into two 9x12-inch baking pans.

Bake at 350 degrees for 35 to 40 minutes or until set. Serve with the Orange Sauce.

Yield: 18 to 20 servings

Orange Sauce

4 whole eggs, or $^1/_2$ cup egg substitute
$^1/_4$ cup Cointreau
$^1/_4$ cup frozen orange juice concentrate, thawed
2 cups confectioners' sugar
1 cup (2 sticks) margarine, melted

Combine the eggs, Cointreau and orange juice concentrate in a food processor. Process until well blended. Add the confectioners' sugar and margarine. Process until smooth.

Yield: 1 quart

Lemon Poppy Seed Bread Pudding

2 cups sugar
1 quart milk
1 quart water
12 eggs, beaten
1 tablespoon lemon flavoring
$1/4$ cup poppy seeds
$1/2$ cup (1 stick) margarine
6 to 8 cups broken poppy seed bread pieces
2 tablespoons lemon zest
Lemon Sauce (page 117)

Combine the sugar, milk and water in a bowl and mix well. Combne the eggs, lemon flavoring, poppy seeds and margarine in a bowl and mix well. Add to the sugar mixture and mix well. Add the bread and lemon zest and mix well. Let stand until the liquid is absorbed. Spoon into two 9×12-inch pans.

Bake at 350 degrees for 35 to 40 minutes or until set. Serve with the Lemon Sauce.

Yield: 18 to 20 servings

Christmas Trifle

1 pound cake
1 small jar raspberry jam
$1/2$ cup sherry
1 (14-ounce) can sweetened condensed milk
1 large package vanilla instant pudding mix
2 cups cold water
2 teaspoons grated lemon zest
8 ounces whipped topping
4 pints strawberries, capped, halved
8 kiwifruit, peeled, thinly sliced
2 cups blueberries
1 cup whipped cream
1 cup toasted slivered almonds
1 cup toasted coconut, optional

Cut the pound cake into halves horizontally. Combine the jam and sherry in a bowl and mix well. Spread evenly over the cut sides of the pound cake. Cut the cake into cubes.

Combine the condensed milk, pudding mix, cold water, lemon zest and whipped topping in a bowl and mix well. Arrange pound cake cubes in the bottom and up the side of a large glass bowl. Spread with some of the condensed milk mixture. Spoon some of the strawberries, kiwifruit and blueberries on top. Repeat the layers using the remaining ingredients. Spread with the whipped cream. Sprinkle with the almonds and coconut.

Yield: 10 to 12 servings.

Cream Cheese Brownies

    3 cups chocolate chips
    3/4 cup (1 1/2 sticks) butter
    8 eggs
    3 cups sugar
    2 cups flour
    2 teaspoons baking powder
    1 teaspoon salt
    1 teaspoon almond extract
    4 teaspoons vanilla extract
    2 cups chopped nuts
    12 ounces cream cheese, softened
    1/2 cup (1 stick) butter
    1 cup sugar
    4 eggs
    1/4 cup flour
    2 teaspoons vanilla extract

Combine the chocolate chips and 3/4 cup butter in a saucepan. Cook over low heat until melted, stirring constantly. Combine 8 eggs and 3 cups sugar in a mixing bowl. Beat until blended. Add 2 cups flour, baking powder, salt, almond extract, 4 teaspoons vanilla and nuts and mix well. Add the chocolate mixture and mix well.

Combine the cream cheese, 1/2 cup butter, 1 cup sugar, 4 eggs, 1/4 cup flour and 2 teaspoons vanilla in a mixing bowl. Beat until smooth. Reserve 1 1/2 cups of the chocolate mixture. Spoon the remaining chocolate mixture into an 18x24-inch baking dish or two 9x12-inch baking dishes. Pour the cream cheese mixture over the chocolate mixture. Drizzle the reserved chocolate mixture over the top. Swirl with a knife to marbleize. Bake at 300 degrees until set, about 40 minutes.

Yield: 15 to 18 servings

Carrot Cake

2 cups flour
2 cups sugar
2 teaspoons baking soda
2 teaspoons salt
2 teaspoons cinnamon
4 eggs
1 cup vegetable oil
4 cups grated carrots (about 1 pound)
1/2 cup chopped pecans
8 ounces cream cheese, softened
1/2 cup (1 stick) butter, softened
1 1/2 pounds sifted confectioners' sugar
1 teaspoon vanilla extract

For the cake, combine the flour, sugar, baking soda, salt and cinnamon in
a bowl and mix well. Beat the eggs in a large mixing bowl until frothy. Beat in the
oil. Add the flour mixture gradually, beating constantly. Beat until smooth. Stir
in the carrots and pecans. Spoon into 2 greased and floured 9-inch cake pans.
Bake at 350 degrees for 35 to 40 minutes. Cool in the pans for 10 minutes.
Remove to wire racks to cool completely.

For the frosting, combine the cream cheese, butter and confectioners' sugar in
a mixing bowl. Beat until smooth. Beat in the vanilla. Spread between the layers
and over the top and side of the cooled cake.

Yield: 12 servings

Chocolate Cake

2 cups sugar
1³/₄ cups flour
³/₄ cup baking cocoa
1¹/₂ teaspoons baking soda
1¹/₂ teaspoons baking powder
1 teaspoon salt
2 eggs
1 cup milk
¹/₂ cup vegetable oil
2 teaspoons vanilla extract
1 cup boiling water
6 tablespoons butter, softened
¹/₃ cup light baking cocoa
¹/₂ cup medium baking cocoa
³/₄ cup dark baking cocoa
2²/₃ cups confectioners' sugar
¹/₃ cup milk
1 teaspoon vanilla extract

For the cake, combine the sugar, flour, ³/₄ cup baking cocoa, baking soda, baking powder and salt in a mixing bowl and mix well.

Add the eggs, 1 cup milk, oil and 2 teaspoons vanilla. Beat until well blended, scraping the side of the bowl. Add the boiling water and mix well.

Chocolate Cake (continued)

Spoon into 3 greased 9-inch cake pans. Bake at 350 degrees for 30 to 35 minutes.

Cool in the pans for 10 minutes. Remove to wire racks to cool completely.

For the frosting, combine the butter, light baking cocoa, medium baking cocoa, dark baking cocoa, confectioners' sugar, $1/3$ cup milk and 1 teaspoon vanilla in a bowl and mix until smooth. Spread between the layers and over the top and side of the cooled cake.

Yield: 12 servings

German Chocolate Cake

4 (1-ounce) squares German's sweet chocolate
$1/2$ cup hot water
1 cup (2 sticks) margarine or butter, softened
4 eggs
$2^1/4$ cups flour
2 cups sugar
1 teaspoon baking soda
$1/2$ teaspoon salt
1 cup buttermilk
1 teaspoon vanilla extract
1 cup sugar
1 cup evaporated milk
$1/2$ cup (1 stick) butter
3 eggs, beaten
$1^1/2$ cups flaked coconut
1 cup chopped pecans
1 teaspoon vanilla extract

For the cake, combine the chocolate and hot water in a bowl and stir until the chocolate is melted. Beat the margarine in a mixing bowl until light and fluffy.

Add 4 eggs 1 at a time, beating well after each addition. Add the flour, 2 cups sugar, baking soda, salt, buttermilk and 1 teaspoon vanilla. Beat at low speed just until mixed.

German Chocolate Cake (continued)

Spoon into 3 greased and floured 9-inch cake pans. Bake at 350 degrees for 35 to 40 minutes or until the cake tests done.

Cool in the pans for 10 minutes. Remove to wire racks to cool completely.

For the frosting, combine 1 cup sugar, evaporated milk, butter and 3 eggs in a saucepan. Cook over medium heat just until bubbly, stirring constantly. Add the coconut, pecans and 1 teaspoon vanilla and mix well.

Let stand to cool until of spreadable consistency. Spread between the layers and over the top of the cooled cake.

Yield: 12 servings

Hummingbird Cake

3 cups flour
2 cups sugar
1 teaspoon salt
1 teaspoon baking soda
1 teaspoon cinnamon
3 eggs
1^1/$_2$ cups vegetable oil
1^1/$_2$ teaspoons vanilla extract
1 (8-ounce) can crushed pineapple
1 cup chopped nuts
2 cups mashed ripe bananas
8 ounces cream cheese, softened
^{1}/$_2$ cup (1 stick) butter, softened
1^1/$_2$ pounds sifted confectioners' sugar
1 teaspoon vanilla extract

For the cake, combine the flour, sugar, salt, baking soda, cinnamon, eggs, oil, 1^1/$_2$ teaspoons vanilla, pineapple, nuts and bananas in a bowl and mix well. Spoon into a greased bundt pan. Bake at 350 degrees for 1 hour or until the cake tests done. Cool in the pan for 10 minutes. Remove to a wire rack to cool completely.

For the frosting, combine the cream cheese, butter and confectioners' sugar in a mixing bowl. Beat until smooth. Beat in 1 teaspoon vanilla. Spread over the top and side of the cooled cake.

Yield: 16 servings

Lemon Squares

4 cups flour
2 cups (4 sticks) butter, softened
1 cup confectioners' sugar
4 cups sugar
8 eggs
4 tablespoons grated lemon zest
$3/4$ cup fresh lemon juice
$1/2$ cup flour
4 teaspoons baking powder
$1/2$ teaspoon salt

Combine 4 cups flour, butter and confectioners' sugar in a bowl and mix well. Spread evenly in an 18×24-inch baking pan. Bake at 350 degrees for 15 minutes or until golden brown. Combine the sugar and eggs in a mixing bowl. Beat until light and fluffy. Add the lemon zest, lemon juice, $1/2$ cup flour, baking powder and salt and mix well. Spoon over the baked crust.

Bake for 15 to 20 minutes or just until set. Let stand to cool completely. Dust with additional confectioners' sugar.

Yield: 15 to 18 servings

Strawberry Dip

2 cups strawberry cream cheese
1 cup confectioners' sugar
$1/2$ cup white wine
1 cup sliced strawberries

Combine the strawberry cream cheese, confectioners' sugar, white wine and strawberries in a food processor. Process until smooth. Chill until serving time. Serve with slices of fresh fruit.

Yield: 4 cups

Tart Lemon Dip

2 cups cream cheese
1 cup confectioners' sugar
$1/2$ cup lemon juice

Combine the cream cheese, confectioners' sugar and lemon juice in a food processor. Process until smooth. Chill until serving time.

Yield: 3 cups

It happened fourteen years ago. I applied for a job and was ready to go. Her name was Norma, and she gave me a call to work at the Café inside the mall. She spoke rather softly and was very polite, as I listened she explained her vision in sight.

A waitress back then, the manager now, I can remember setting up boarding house style. We moved all the tables and chairs to the back. No one could believe how Norma's was packed. People were standing in line for hours, hoping to get the chance to nibble or devour. Chicken salad, gumbo, poppy seed bread, and more. Most just wanted to get bread pudding out the door.

Kathie cashiered on that busy day. My head seemed to spin as the time rolled away. Gerry, her husband, came in with a smile. He helped me count my "loot," which made it worthwhile.

Marketbasket, Thanksgiving, and Christmas came and went. Can you believe we've been that busy ever since? I never dreamed she would be such a success. She's hard-working, strong, and has a matching dress.

Norma, you're great! Thanks for the years. When I think back on the memories, I have to wipe away the tears. May Norma's live on for many more years.

Much love, —Jo

When asked to write a memory for this cookbook, all I could think was "which one?" Because after 12 years there are many (good and bad)! One that really sticks out in my mind was a catering job Norma's was asked to do Christmas of 1994 at Elebash Jewelry Store. When asked to help, I said yes for two reasons. First, I have always enjoyed the catering part of the restaurant business the best. Second, this wasn't the first time doing this for Elebash's, as we had catered this particular function for several years.

Everything was going as usual until Norma informed everyone working that they had to go to the costume store and get a dress from the Civil War period to wear. Elebash's was honoring two new businesses downtown, The Civil War Museum, and Norma's On the Run. Well, of course, we all thought we would feel like Scarlett O'Hara for a night. No one knew what the other dresses looked like until we arrived that night. Boy, did we laugh at each other, as none of us looked like Scarlett, rather more like Mammy and Prissy!

As we waited for Norma to arrive and see what her dress looked like, we sure got a shock when she walked in smiling and wearing a stylish black dress (what we normally wear for catering). She politely said, "You didn't think I was going to wear that, did you?"

We learned to always ask what the attire was before committing to an after-hours job. Anyway, it was a fun night that will always make me laugh when thought of, and I do thank Norma for all my memories, good and bad.

—Kathie

In Memoriam

On August 1, 2001, my dad died. It was the thirteenth anniversary of the opening of Norma's Café. It was also the second week of a pay period. For thirteen years, Dad prepared my payroll hours every other week. When he died unexpectedly, I was faced with arranging a funeral, consoling my mom, dealing with my own grief, and preparing my payroll as usual. Many offers to help with payroll were extended and refused. I felt it was my responsibility to complete this task.

As I returned home after the funeral, the pay sheets awaited me. I was totally unable to open my dad's folder and calculate hours worked. After noticing my reticence, my oldest daugher, Meghan, stepped in and offered to do the job for me. My ever-confident child knew I needed help with this chore. She assured me she knew how to do it "like Granddaddy did." I gladly accepted her offer and felt relieved until thirty minutes later. My precious child, who wanted to help me, was in tears. "I can't do it either Mama," she said. A simple job—calculating hours worked—and two intelligent women could not do it.

At that point, we hugged and sat head-to-head and did the pay sheets together. The task itself was simple; replacing the person who had done it for so many years was not. My child and I realized then how much we were going to miss Granddaddy.

—Norma

As we celebrate...

As we celebrate fourteen years at Norma's and debut our closely held recipes in *As Always*, again I say thank you to my family, my fellow workers, and our many customers who are the real reason for our success.

Index

Sausage Bake, 108
Vegetable Soufflé, 109

Fruit. *See also* Apple; Apricot; Coconut;
Cranberry; Lemon; Orange;
Pineapple; Pumpkin; Raspberry
Christmas Trifle, 123
Fiesta Bread Pudding, 120
Fresh Fruit Cobbler, 112
Hummingbird Cake, 130
Mama Muffins, 101
Strawberry Dip, 132
Tart Lemon Dip, 132

Ham
Broccoli, Ham and Berry
Salad, 21
Cheesy Ham and Potato Chowder, 39
Ham and Asparagus Crepes, 79
Ham and Cheese Strata, 105
Ham and Corn Soup, 42
Ham and Potato Chowder, 39
Ham Pinwheels, 106
Jambalaya Salad, 18
Piquant Cheese Loaf, 103
Red Beans, 80
Split Pea Soup, 53
Vegetable Soup, 41

Lemon
Flavored Sauce, 117
Lemon Bread, 93
Lemon Poppy Seed Bread
Pudding, 122
Lemon Squares, 131
Tart Lemon Dip, 132

Mushrooms
Chicken and Artichoke
Casserole, 60
Chicken and Wild Rice, 66
Chicken Marsala, 65
Marinated Beef and Mushroom
Salad, 20
Marinated Chicken Salad, 12

Mushroom Soup, 48
Seafood Bisque, 51
Shrimp and Mushroom Crepes, 79
Shrimp and Mushroom Vin Blanc, 75
Shrimp and Wild Rice Casserole, 76
Shrimp with Mushroom
Sauce, 74
Tortellini Salad, 27

Orange
Cranberry Bread, 91
Fiesta Bread Pudding, 120
Mandarin Chicken and Rice
Salad, 16
Orange Chicken, 71
Orange Sauce, 121
Oven French Toast, 102

Pasta. *See also* Salads, Pasta
Chicken and Bows Soup, 35
Chicken Italiano, 64
Chicken Italiano Soup, 35
Chicken Marsala, 65
Chicken Noodle Soup, 34
Chicken Pasta Soup, 34
Dill Vegetables and Pasta, 77
Italian Tomato Soup, 40
Tomato Tortellini Soup, 40

Pineapple
Hummingbird Cake, 130
Oriental Chicken Salad, 17
Pumpkin Bread, 94

Pork. *See* Ham; Sausage

Potatoes
Beef Burgundy Stew, 58
Cheesy Ham and Potato
Chowder, 39
Chicken Chowder, 35
Ham and Potato Chowder, 39
Potato Chowder, 39

Poultry. *See* Chicken; Turkey

Shrimp and Mushroom Vin
  Blanc, 75
Shrimp and Shells Salad, 25
Shrimp and Wild Rice Casserole, 76
Shrimp Florentine, 73
Shrimp with Mushroom Sauce, 74

Soups
Beer Cheese Soup, 50
Cheesy Broccoli Soup, 47
Cheesy Cauliflower Soup, 46
Cheesy Ham and Potato
  Chowder, 39
Chicken and Bows Soup, 35
Chicken and Rice Soup, 34
Chicken and Wild Rice Soup, 34
Chicken Chowder, 35
Chicken Florentine Soup, 35
Chicken Italiano Soup, 35
Chicken Noodle Soup, 34
Chicken Pasta Soup, 34
Chicken Vegetable Soup, 34
Crab Chowder, 52
Cream of Artichoke Soup, 37
Cream of Broccoli Soup, 47
Cream of Cauliflower Soup, 44
Cream of Celery Soup, 38
Cream of Chicken Soup, 35
Cream of Onion Soup, 49
Cream of Spinach Soup, 45
Cream of Tomato Soup, 40
Creamy Corn Soup, 42
Curried Pumpkin Soup, 54
Ham and Corn Soup, 42
Ham and Potato Chowder, 39
Italian Tomato Soup, 40
Mushroom Soup, 48
Norma's Chicken Soup, 34
Norma's Seafood Gumbo, 36
Onion Soup, 49
Pepper Corn Soup, 42
Potato Chowder, 39
Seafood Bisque, 51
Shrimp and Corn Soup, 42
Split Pea Soup, 53

Tomato Florentine Soup, 40
Tomato Tortellini Soup, 40
Tomato Vegetable Soup, 40
Vegetable Soup, 41
Zucchini Carrot Soup, 43

Spinach
Chicken and Artichoke Salad, 13
Chicken Florentine Soup, 35
Cream of Spinach Soup, 45
Oriental Chicken Salad, 17
Shrimp Florentine, 73
Tomato Florentine Soup, 40

Squash
Burgundy Beef Salad, 19
Chicken Pasta Salad, 14
Tortellini Salad, 27

Turkey
Turkey and Wild Rice Salad, 22

Vegetables. *See also* Artichokes; Beans;
  Broccoli; Carrots; Cauliflower; Corn;
  Mushrooms; Potatoes; Spinach;
  Squash; Zucchini
Chicken Vegetable Soup, 34
Dill Vegetables and Pasta, 77
Ham and Asparagus Crepes, 79
Primavera Crepes, 79
Quiche, 107
Split Pea Soup, 53
Tomato Vegetable Soup, 40
Vegetable Soufflé, 109
Vegetable Soup, 41

Zucchini
Burgundy Beef Salad, 19
Chicken Pasta Salad, 14
Tortellini Salad, 27
Zucchini Carrot Soup, 43

Contributors

Photo Courtesy Paul White Photography

Seated: Karen Stewart, Joneida Heckler, Norma Murray, Sharon Hazzard, Stacey Hazzard

Standing: Caitlin Murray, Kathie Sutton, Stella Long, Destiny Mosley, Priscilla Knight, Norma Jean Southard, Patricia Robinson, Meghan Murray Moorhouse

As Always

Norma Fleming Murray

Norma's On the Run

28 North Palafox Street

Pensacola, Florida 32501

Telephone 1-850-434-8646

Fax 1-850-934-9586

E-mail normascookbook@earthlink.net

YOUR ORDER	QTY	TOTAL
As Always at $24.95 per book		$
Florida residents add $1.87 sales tax per book		$
Postage and handling at $3.50 per book		$
	TOTAL	$

_____

Name

_____

Address

_____

City   State   Zip

_____

Telephone

Method of Payment: [   ] Visa   [   ] MasterCard   [   ] American Express
                    [   ] Check payable to *As Always*

_____

Account Number   Expiration Date

_____

Signature

Photocopies will be accepted.